**DK** BACKPACK BOOKS

# 1,001 FACTS ABOUT SPACE

D0095870

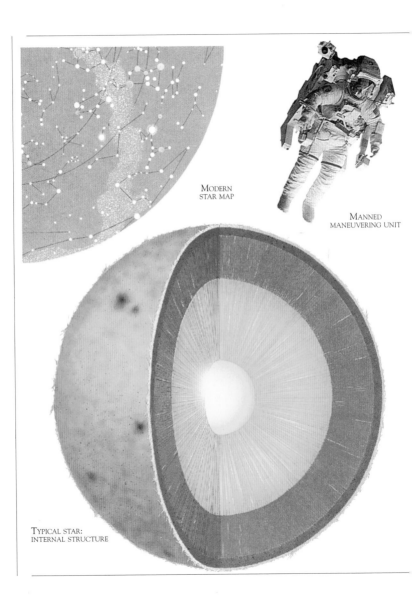

MODERN
STAR MAP

MANNED
MANEUVERING UNIT

TYPICAL STAR:
INTERNAL STRUCTURE

# BACKPACK BOOKS

# 1,001 FACTS ABOUT SPACE

Written by
CAROLE STOTT and
CLINT TWIST

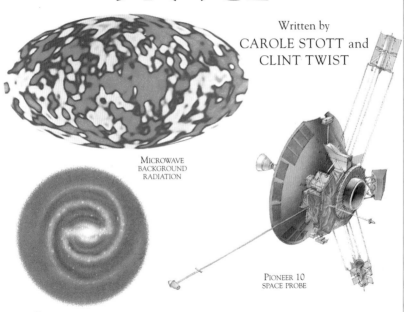

MICROWAVE
BACKGROUND
RADIATION

PIONEER 10
SPACE PROBE

BARRED SPIRAL GALAXY

DK PUBLISHING, INC.

LONDON, NEW YORK, MUNICH,
MELBOURNE AND DELHI

| | |
|---:|:---|
| **Editor** | Simon Mugford |
| **Designer** | Dan Green |
| **Senior editor** | Andrew Macintyre |
| **Design manager** | Jane Thomas |
| **DTP design** | Jill Bunyan |
| **Production** | Nicola Torode |

With thanks to the original team

| | |
|---:|:---|
| **Project editor** | Clint Twist |
| **Art editor** | Alexandra Brown |
| **Senior editor** | Laura Buller |
| **Senior art editor** | Helen Senior |
| **Picture research** | Fiona Watson |
| **Production** | Louise Barratt |

First American Edition, 2002

2468109753

Published in the United States by
DK Publishing, Inc.,
375 Hudson Street,
New York, NY 10014

A catalog record for this book is available from
the Library of Congress

ISBN 0-7894-8450-1

Color reproduction by Colourscan
Printed and bound in Singapore

See our complete product line at
www.dk.com

# Contents

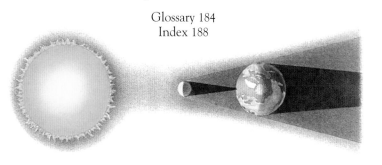

# UNIVERSE

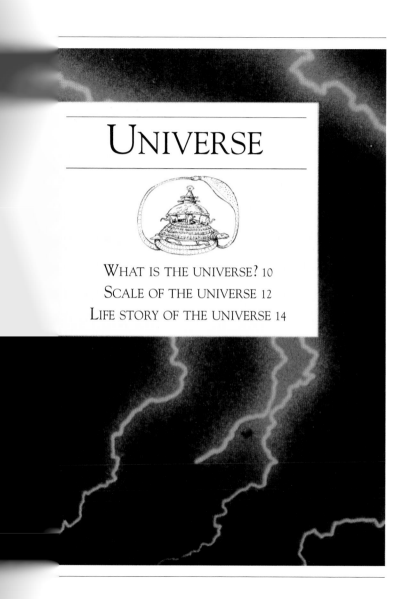

# WHAT IS THE UNIVERSE?

THE UNIVERSE IS EVERYTHING that exists. From the Earth beneath our feet to the farthest stars, everything is a part of the universe. The universe is so large that it contains countless billions of stars. However, most of it consists of nothing but empty space.

*Galaxies*

*Comet – a dirty snowball*

*Galaxy containing billions of stars*

*Supernova – the death of a large star*

LOOKING TO THE SKIES

From Earth, we can look into space and study the universe. In every direction we look there are stars. There are more stars in the universe than any other type of object – stars at different stages of their lives in enormous groups called galaxies, including at least one star that has planets. Despite the huge size of the universe, we know of only one place where life exists – planet Earth.

UNIVERSE FACTS

• There are about 100 billion galaxies in the universe; each contains more than 100 billion stars.

• The most distant objects we can detect are 87,000 million million million miles (139,000 million million million km) away.

## HORSEHEAD IN SPACE

Looking like a chess knight, the Horsehead Nebula (center left) is a gigantic cloud of dark-colored dust. It is visible because the dust blocks out light from behind the nebula, so that we see it in silhouette. The universe contains many similar clouds that block our view of different regions.

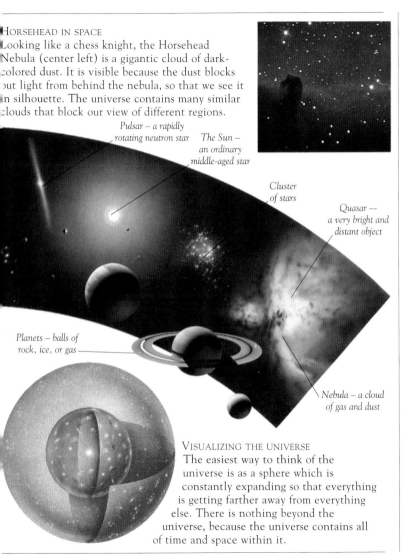

*Pulsar – a rapidly rotating neutron star*

*The Sun – an ordinary middle-aged star*

*Cluster of stars*

*Quasar – a very bright and distant object*

*Planets – balls of rock, ice, or gas*

*Nebula – a cloud of gas and dust*

## VISUALIZING THE UNIVERSE

The easiest way to think of the universe is as a sphere which is constantly expanding so that everything is getting farther away from everything else. There is nothing beyond the universe, because the universe contains all of time and space within it.

# SCALE OF THE UNIVERSE

DISTANCES IN THE UNIVERSE are so great that the light-year is used as a unit of measurement. Light travels at about 186,000 miles/sec (300,000 km/s), and a light-year (ly) is the distance light travels in one year. A galaxy can measure thousands of light-years across and be millions of light-years distant.

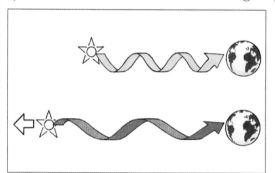

LIGHT AND MOTION
A star's light can tell us about its motion. If the star is moving away from Earth, its light is stretched by comparison with stationary stars. Light from a star moving away is also shifted toward the red end of the spectrum. Stars approaching Earth have compressed light shifted toward blue.

SCALE OF SIZES
The human world, the world of everyday experience, is dwarfed by the scale of the universe. Earth is one of nine planets orbiting the Sun, which is one of about 200 billion stars in the Milky Way galaxy.

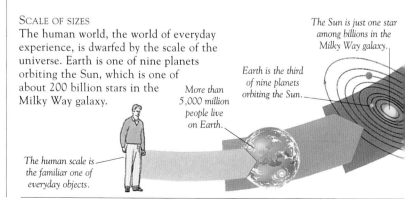

*The Sun is just one star among billions in the Milky Way galaxy.*

*Earth is the third of nine planets orbiting the Sun.*

*More than 5,000 million people live on Earth.*

*The human scale is the familiar one of everyday objects.*

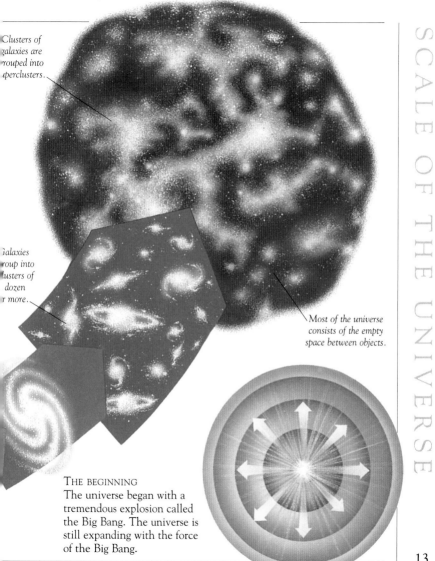

Clusters of
galaxies are
grouped into
superclusters.

Galaxies
group into
clusters of
a dozen
or more.

Most of the universe
consists of the empty
space between objects.

THE BEGINNING
The universe began with a
tremendous explosion called
the Big Bang. The universe is
still expanding with the force
of the Big Bang.

# LIFE STORY OF THE UNIVERSE

ALL MATTER, ENERGY, space, and time were created in the Big Bang around 15 billion years ago. At first the universe was small and very hot. Atomic particles joined to form hydrogen and helium and the universe expanded and cooled. Over millions of years these gases have produced galaxies, stars, planets, and us.

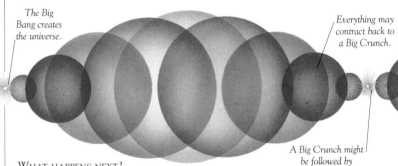

*The Big Bang creates the universe.*

*Everything may contract back to a Big Crunch.*

*A Big Crunch might be followed by another Big Bang.*

WHAT HAPPENS NEXT?
There are two theories about the future of the universe. Either it will stop expanding and shrink back in a process called a Big Crunch, or carry on expanding forever.

BIG BANG RIPPLES
This map of the whole sky is based on tiny variations in the temperature of space. Red is warmer than average and blue is colder. These tiny variations are irregularities of the Big Bang explosion. The information for the map was obtained by the Cosmic Background Explorer Satellite (COBE).

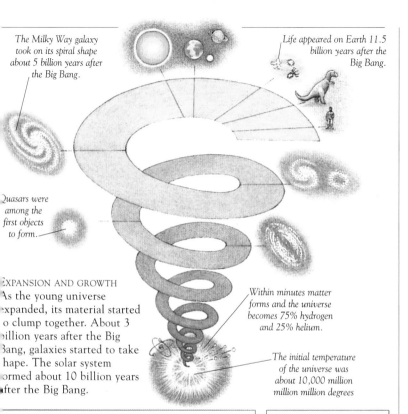

*The Milky Way galaxy took on its spiral shape about 5 billion years after the Big Bang.*

*Life appeared on Earth 11.5 billion years after the Big Bang.*

*Quasars were among the first objects to form.*

*Within minutes matter forms and the universe becomes 75% hydrogen and 25% helium.*

*The initial temperature of the universe was about 10,000 million million million degrees*

## EXPANSION AND GROWTH

As the young universe expanded, its material started to clump together. About 3 billion years after the Big Bang, galaxies started to take shape. The solar system formed about 10 billion years after the Big Bang.

UNIVERSE: COOLING DATA

| Time after Big Bang | Temperature |
|---|---|
| $10^{-6}$ secs | $1.8 \times 10^{13}$°F ($10^{13}$°C) |
| 3 minutes | $1.8 \times 10^{8}$°F ($10^{8}$°C) |
| 300,000 years | 10,000°C-18,000°F ($10^{4}$°C) |
| 1 million years | 5,400°F (3,000°C) |
| 1,000 million years | −275°F (−170°C) |
| 15,000 million years | −454°F (−270°C) |

UNIVERSE FACT

• Scientists can trace the life story of the universe back to what is called the Planck time, $10^{-43}$ seconds after the Big Bang. $10^{-43}$ means a decimal point followed by 42 zeros and then a one.

# GALAXIES

# WHAT IS A GALAXY?

A GALAXY IS an enormous group of stars. A large galaxy may have a billion, a small galaxy only a few hundred thousand. Even small galaxies are so big that it takes light thousands of years to cross them. Galaxies are formed from vast spinning clouds of gas. Many continue to spin. The speed of rotation affects their shape.

DISTANT STAR CITY
The Andromeda galaxy is so far away that its light takes 2,200,000 years to travel to Earth. We see the galaxy as it was 2,200,000 years ago.

GALAXIES: THE FOUR BASIC TYPES

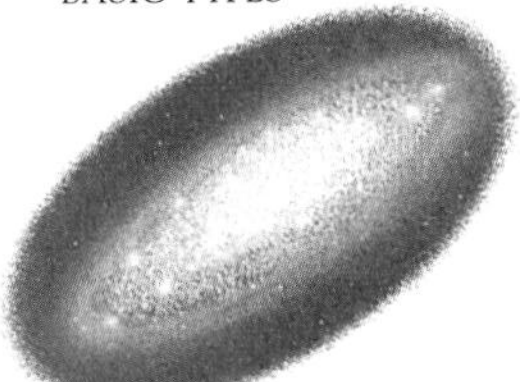

ELLIPTICAL
These range from ball-shaped to egg-shaped. They contain mainly old stars, and are the most common type.

SPIRAL
These are disk-shaped. Most material is in the spiral arms where new stars are formed. Old stars are in the nucleus.

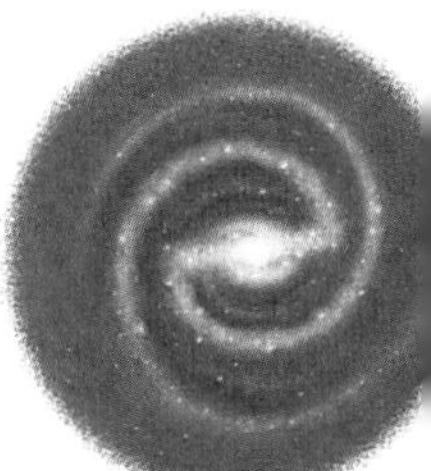

BARRED-SPIRAL
These are like spiral galaxies, but the nucl
is elongated into a ba
The spiral arms exter
from the ends of the

**BRIGHTEST LIGHTS**
This is an X-ray image of a quasi-stellar object, one of the brightest, and remotest objects. The most distant are about 15 billion light-years away. Known as quasars, they are probably the cores of the first galaxies to be formed.

| BRIGHT GALAXIES: DATA | | |
| Galaxy | Distance | Type |
| --- | --- | --- |
| Andromeda (M31) | 2,200,000 ly | Sb |
| M32 | 2,300,000 ly | E2 |
| M33 | 2,400,000 ly | Sc |
| Wolf-Lundmark | 4,290,000 ly | Irr |
| M81 | 9,450,000 ly | Sb |
| Centaurus A | 13,040,000 ly | E0 |
| Pinwheel (M101) | 23,790,000 ly | Sc |
| Whirlpool (M51) | 29,340,000 ly | Sc |
| NGC2841 | 37,490,000 ly | Sb |
| NGC1023 | 39,120,000 ly | E7 |
| NGC3184 | 42,380,000 ly | Sc |
| NGC5866 | 42,380,000 ly | E6 |
| M100 | 48,900,000 ly | Sc |
| NGC6643 | 74,980,000 ly | Sc |
| M77 | 81,500,000 ly | Sb |
| NGC3938 | 94,540,000 ly | Sc |
| NGC2207 | 114,100,000 ly | Sc |

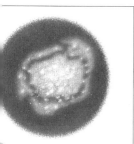

**IRREGULAR**
Some of these have a hint of spiral structure, while others do not fit any known pattern. They are the rarest type.

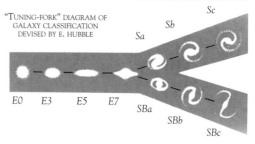

"TUNING-FORK" DIAGRAM OF
GALAXY CLASSIFICATION
DEVISED BY E. HUBBLE

Sc

Sb

Sa

E0   E3   E5   E7
SBa
SBb
SBc

**CLASSIFYING GALAXIES BY SHAPE**
Elliptical galaxies are classified from E0 (spherical) to E7 (very flattened). Spirals (S) and barred spirals (SB) are graded from a to c, according to the compactness of the central nucleus and the tightness of the arms. Irregular galaxies (Irr) are not shown here, but can be divided into types I and II.

GALAXIES

# CLUSTERS AND SUPERCLUSTERS

GALAXIES OCCUR TOGETHER in
clusters that range in size from
a few to a few thousand galaxies.
Clusters themselves also occur
in groups called superclusters,
which are the largest structures
in the universe.

NEIGHBORING CLUSTER
The Virgo cluster is about 60
million light-years away, but
it is the nearest major cluster
to our own Local Group.

THE LOCAL GROUP
Our own cluster is
about five million
light-years across
and contains about
30 galaxies. The
largest galaxies in
the Local Group are
Andromeda (M31),
Triangulum (M33),
and our own Milky
Way galaxy.

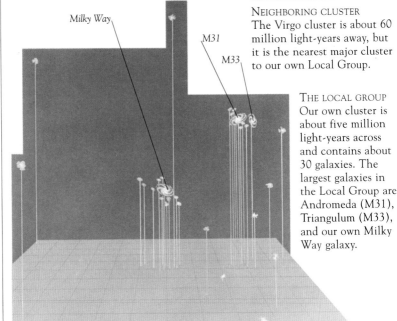

Milky Way

M31

M33

SOME LOCAL GROUP GALAXIES: DATA

| Name | Diameter | Distance |
| --- | --- | --- |
| Andromeda | 150,000 ly | 2,200,000 ly |
| M33 | 40,000 ly | 2,400,000 ly |
| Large Magellanic Cloud (LMC) | 30,000 ly | 170,000 ly |
| Small Magellanic Cloud (SMC) | 20,000 ly | 190,000 ly |
| NGC 6822 | 15,000 ly | 1,800,000 ly |
| NGC 205 | 11,000 ly | 2,200,000 ly |

HONEYCOMB SPACE

Superclusters tend to be flattened into disks or sheets, or elongated into filaments. These shapes cannot be seen through a telescope, but scientists now know that the large-scale structure of the universe is basically a honeycomb arrangement. Superclusters are arranged on the surface of immense "bubbles." These bubbles are almost completely empty of matter. They are huge voids that contain only a few atoms of gas.

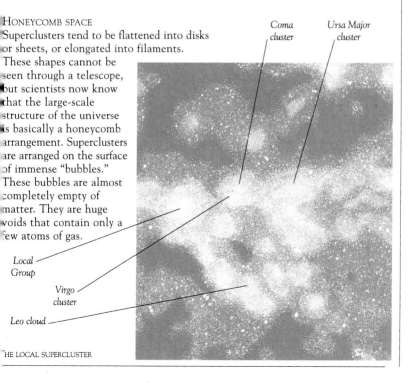

Coma cluster

Ursa Major cluster

Local Group

Virgo cluster

Leo cloud

THE LOCAL SUPERCLUSTER

# THE MILKY WAY

THE SUN IS JUST ONE of the more than 100 billion stars in our own galaxy – the Milky Way. Ours is a spiral galaxy, with a nucleus of old stars surrounded by a halo of even older stars. All the young stars are located in the spiral arms. The Milky Way is so large that it takes light 100,000 years to travel from edge to edge. All the stars we see at night are in the Milky Way.

SAGITTARIUS STAR CLOUD
This photograph shows young stars in a small part of the Sagittarius arm of the Milky Way. Clouds of dust obscure our view of most of that region of the galaxy.

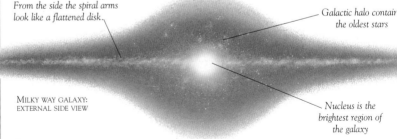

*From the side the spiral arms look like a flattened disk.*

*Galactic halo contain the oldest stars*

MILKY WAY GALAXY:
EXTERNAL SIDE VIEW

*Nucleus is the brightest region of the galaxy*

SIDE-ON SPIRAL
Viewed from the side, from a distance of about a million light-years, the Milky Way galaxy would look like a giant lens – with flattened edges and a bright central nucleus. Around the nucleus is a roughly spherical halo that contains the oldest stars in the galaxy.

THE MILKY WAY
AS SEEN FROM
EARTH

ABOVE THE SPIRAL
From above, or below, the spiral arms of
the Milky Way galaxy would be clearly
visible. These contain most of the galaxy's
gas and dust, and this is where
star-forming regions
are found.

MILKY WAY FACTS
• Some astronomers
think the Milky Way is
a barred spiral galaxy.
• Our galaxy rotates.
The Sun takes about
220 million years to
make one revolution –
a period sometimes
known as a "cosmic
year." Stars in other
parts of the galaxy
travel at different rates.

Crux-Centaurus arm

Galactic
nucleus

Location of
the solar system

Orion arm
(Local Arm)

Sagittarius
arm

MILKY WAY GALAXY:
EXTERNAL OVERHEAD VIEW

23

# THE LOCAL ARM

THE SOLAR SYSTEM is situated about two-thirds of the way from the galaxy's center, at the edge of a spiral arm called the Local Arm or the Orion Arm. From this viewpoint, we see the galaxy as a great milky river of stars across the night sky.

*The galactic nucleus is more than 15,000 ly acro*

POSITION OF THE
LOCAL ARM IN
THE GALAXY

### SEVEN STARRY SISTERS

The Pleiades is a cluster of bright stars, seven of which can be seen with the naked eye, hence their popular name – the Seven Sisters – which has been in use for at least 2,000 years. In fact there are more than 200 stars in the cluster, which formed about 60 million years ago – shortly after the dinosaurs died out on Earth.

SPECTACULAR END

The Dumbbell Nebula, located about 1,000 light-years from the Sun, is a single star nearing the end of its life. Spherical shells of gas are blown out from the star's surface, making a spectacular sight. Gradually the gas will disperse, and will eventually be used to form new stars elsewhere in the galaxy.

LOCAL ARM FACTS

• From edge to edge the Dumbbell Nebula is two light-years in diameter.

• Some stars in Canis Major are only about 300,000 years old – mere star babies compared with our 5 billion-year-old Sun.

• The nearest bright star cluster to the Sun is the Hyades about 150 light-years away. The Hyades forms the V-shape of the bull's head in the constellation of Taurus.

THE LOCAL REGION OF SPACE WITHIN 1,000 LIGHT-YEARS OF THE SUN

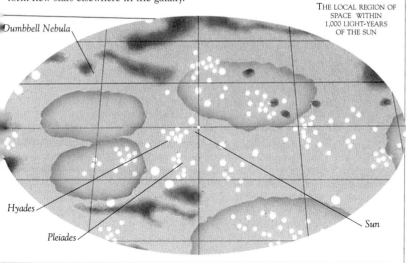

Dumbbell Nebula

Hyades

Pleiades

Sun

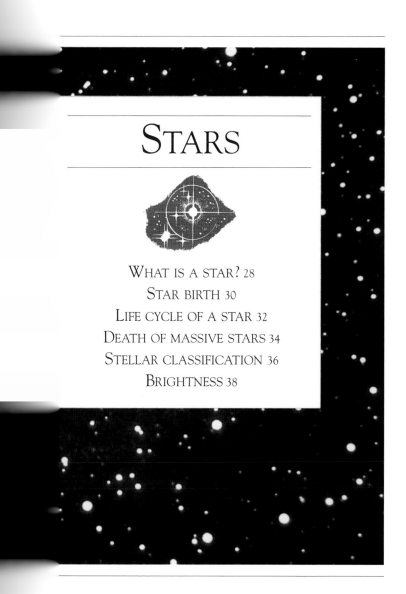

# STARS

# WHAT IS A STAR?

A STAR IS an enormous spinning ball of hot and luminous gas. Most stars contain two main gases – hydrogen and helium. These gases are held together by gravity, and at the core they are very densely packed. Within the core, immense amounts of energy are produced.

STAR CLUSTER
The cluster M13 in the constellation of Hercules contains hundreds of thousands of stars arranged in a compact ball.

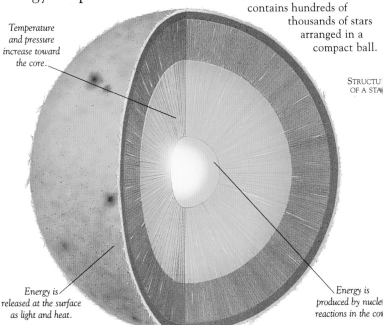

STRUCTU
OF A STA

*Temperature and pressure increase toward the core.*

*Energy is released at the surface as light and heat.*

*Energy is produced by nucle reactions in the co*

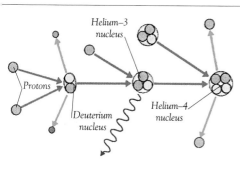

## CORE FUSION

A star produces energy by nuclear fusion. Within the core, hydrogen nuclei (protons) collide and fuse to form first deuterium (heavy hydrogen) and then two forms of helium. During fusion, energy is given off. This type of reaction, which is found in most stars, is called the proton-proton chain.

VARYING SIZES

Stars differ greatly in the amount of gas they contain, and in their size. The largest stars are 1,000 times the diameter of the Sun, while the smallest are just a fraction of its size – not much bigger than the planet Jupiter.

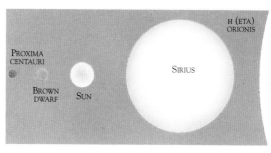

PROMINENT STARS: DATA

| Name | Designation | Distance |
| --- | --- | --- |
| Vega | α Lyrae | 26 ly |
| Pollux | β Geminorum | 36 ly |
| Capella | α Aurigae | 45 ly |
| Aldebaran | α Tauri | 68 ly |
| Regulus | α Leonis | 84 ly |
| Canopus | α Carinae | 98 ly |
| Spica | α Virginis | 260 ly |
| Betelgeuse | α Orionis | 520 ly |
| Polaris | α Ursa Minoris | 700 ly |

### STAR FACTS

• All the chemical elements heavier than hydrogen, helium, and lithium were made by nuclear reactions inside stars.

• The mass of the Sun – 1 solar mass – is used as a standard for measuring other stars.

# STAR BIRTH

STARS FOLLOW a life cycle that
lasts millions to billions of
years. All stars begin in the
same way – as material in a
nebula, a cloud of gas and dust.
Stars are not born individually,
but in groups called clusters.
Initially, the stars in a cluster
have roughly the same
composition. Despite these
early similarities, the stars
usually develop at different
rates, and most clusters drift
apart before very long.

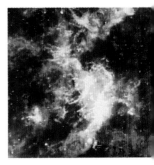

STELLAR BIRTHPLACE
In the Orion Nebula light
from new stars illuminates
the dust clouds. The stars
themselves remain hidden
by the dust. One of these
young stars is 10,000 times
brighter than the Sun.

FORMATION AND EARLY DEVELOPMENT
OF A STAR

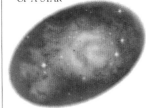

Inside a nebula, gravity
causes spinning balls of
gas to form – these are
known as protostars.

The protostar (seen here
in cross-section) shrinks,
and its core becomes
denser. An outer halo of
gas and dust develops.

When the core reache
critical density, nuclea
reactions start. The
energy released blows
away most of the halo

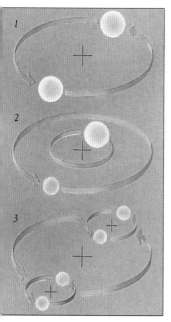

## SINGLE OR DOUBLE

The Sun is unusual – it is a solitary star. In most cases a protostar spins fast enough to form a double or multiple star (1). Multiple stars may orbit around a common center of gravity (2), and may also orbit around one another (3). Double stars often appear to be variable in their light output because one star regularly blocks the light of the other.

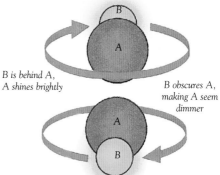

B is behind A, A shines brightly

B obscures A, making A seem dimmer

As the young star continues to spin rapidly, the remaining gas and dust become flattened into a disk.

In at least one case (the star we call the Sun) this disk of gas and dust has formed into a system of orbiting planets.

With or without planets, the new star now shines steadily, converting hydrogen to helium by nuclear fusion.

31

# LIFE CYCLE OF A STAR

A STAR'S LIFE CYCLE depends on its mass. Stars of the same mass as the Sun shine steadily for about 10 billion years. More massive stars convert their hydrogen more quickly, and have shorter lives. The Sun is halfway through its life. In about 5 billion years, it will expand to become a red giant star, and then collapse and end as a dwarf star.

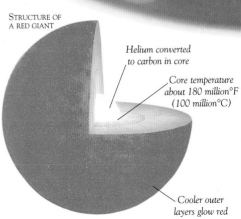

*Star converting hydrogen i.e. in the main sequence*

STRUCTURE OF A RED GIANT

*Helium converted to carbon in core*

*Core temperature about 180 million°F (100 million°C)*

*Cooler outer layers glow red*

RED GIANTS
When most of the hydrogen has been converted to helium, the star becomes a red giant – converting helium to carbon. The core heats up causing the surface to expand and cool. A red giant may expand to more than 100 times its former size.

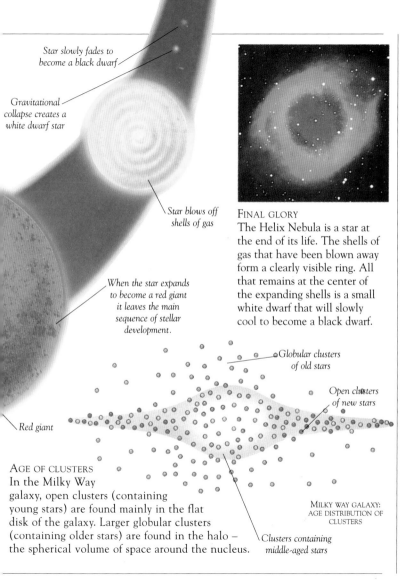

*Star slowly fades to become a black dwarf*

*Gravitational collapse creates a white dwarf star*

*Star blows off shells of gas*

*When the star expands to become a red giant it leaves the main sequence of stellar development.*

*Red giant*

FINAL GLORY
The Helix Nebula is a star at the end of its life. The shells of gas that have been blown away form a clearly visible ring. All that remains at the center of the expanding shells is a small white dwarf that will slowly cool to become a black dwarf.

*Globular clusters of old stars*

*Open clusters of new stars*

AGE OF CLUSTERS
In the Milky Way galaxy, open clusters (containing young stars) are found mainly in the flat disk of the galaxy. Larger globular clusters (containing older stars) are found in the halo – the spherical volume of space around the nucleus.

MILKY WAY GALAXY: AGE DISTRIBUTION OF CLUSTERS

*Clusters containing middle-aged stars*

# DEATH OF MASSIVE STARS

THE WAY A STAR DIES depends on its mass. The most massive stars end their lives by simply exploding. This huge explosion is called a supernova, and may be bright enough to briefly outshine an entire galaxy. What happens next depends on how much stellar material is left after the supernova.

EXPLOSIVE COLLAPSE
Stars of at least eight solar masses end as supernovae. Gravity causes them to collapse with incredible force producing shock waves.

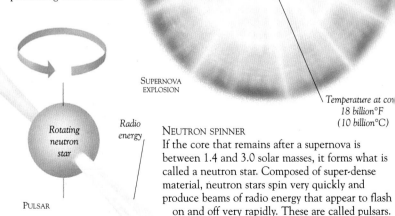

SUPERNOVA
EXPLOSION

Temperature at cor
18 billion°F
(10 billion°C)

Rotating
neutron
star

Radio
energy

PULSAR

NEUTRON SPINNER
If the core that remains after a supernova is between 1.4 and 3.0 solar masses, it forms what is called a neutron star. Composed of super-dense material, neutron stars spin very quickly and produce beams of radio energy that appear to flash on and off very rapidly. These are called pulsars.

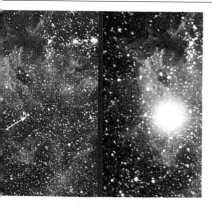

A RARE AND SPECTACULAR SIGHT
Although supernovae are fairly common in the universe, they are rarely seen from Earth. In 1987 a supernova was observed in the Large Magellanic Cloud, a nearby galaxy. The left-hand photograph shows the normal appearance of the star (arrowed). The supernova (designated SN 1987A) is clearly visible in the right-hand picture. After shining brightly for a few months, it slowly faded from view.

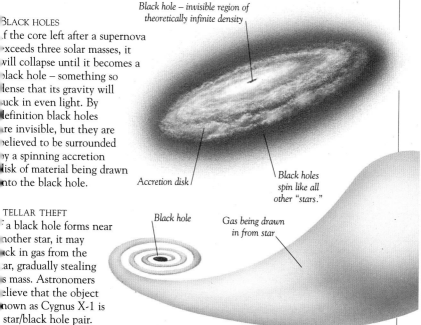

*Black hole – invisible region of theoretically infinite density*

BLACK HOLES
If the core left after a supernova exceeds three solar masses, it will collapse until it becomes a black hole – something so dense that its gravity will suck in even light. By definition black holes are invisible, but they are believed to be surrounded by a spinning accretion disk of material being drawn into the black hole.

*Accretion disk*

*Black holes spin like all other "stars."*

STELLAR THEFT
If a black hole forms near another star, it may suck in gas from the star, gradually stealing its mass. Astronomers believe that the object known as Cygnus X-1 is a star/black hole pair.

*Black hole*

*Gas being drawn in from star*

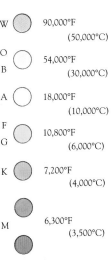

# STELLAR CLASSIFICATION

THE MASS OF A STAR affects its other properties – its color, temperature, and luminosity. Each star is different, but by studying their properties, astronomers have been able to devise a system that enables them to classify all stars.

| | |
|---|---|
| W | 90,000°F (50,000°C) |
| O B | 54,000°F (30,000°C) |
| A | 18,000°F (10,000°C) |
| F G | 10,800°F (6,000°C) |
| K | 7,200°F (4,000°C) |
| M | 6,300°F (3,500°C) |

HEAT AND LIGHT
A star's color is usually a good indicator of its temperature. Blue stars are the hottest, and red the coolest. The Harvard system uses letters of the alphabet to classify stars according to their surface temperature. This diagram shows the color and temperature range of the main types.

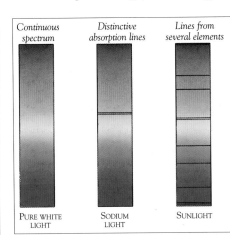

Continuous spectrum — PURE WHITE LIGHT

Distinctive absorption lines — SODIUM LIGHT

Lines from several elements — SUNLIGHT

CHEMICAL LINES
Each star emits its own particular light. Splitting this light into a spectrum reveals the chemical elements that make up the star. The different elements are indicated by dark absorption lines that run across the spectrum. Sodium atoms absorb light only in the yellow part of the spectrum. Sunlight displays hundreds of absorption lines, but only the most prominent are shown here.

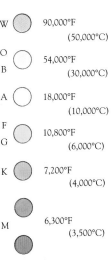

STARS

Supergiant stars e.g. Deneb

Main sequence stars, e.g. Sirius A, which convert hydrogen to helium

Betelgeuse is a red supergiant.

Arcturus is a red giant.

White dwarf stars e.g. Sirius B

Barnard's Star is a main sequence red dwarf.

## COLOR-CODED DIAGRAM

The HR diagram plots a star's temperature against its absolute magnitude (the amount of light it gives off). The brightest stars are at the top, and the dimmest are near the bottom. The hottest stars are to the left and the coolest to the right. Most stars spend some part of their lives in the main sequence which runs from top left to bottom right across the diagram. Giant stars are found above the main sequence and dwarf stars below.

### STAR FACTS

• The hottest type W stars are very rare and are also known as Wolf-Rayet stars.

• By the standards of space, the Sun is very small. Astronomers refer to it as a type G dwarf star.

• Clusters of types O and B stars (known as OB1 clusters) contain hot, bright, young stars.

STELLAR CLASSIFICATION

# BRIGHTNESS

HOW BRIGHTLY A STAR shines in the sky depends on its luminosity (amount of light energy produced), and on its distance from Earth. Astronomers use two different scales to measure a star's magnitude (brightness). Absolute magnitude compares stars from a standard distance. Apparent magnitude describes how bright a star appears as viewed from Earth.

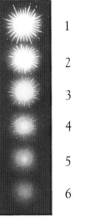

1
2
3
4
5
6

OBSERVED BRIGHTNESS
The scale of apparent magnitude for naked-eye stars. Brighter stars have lower numerical values.

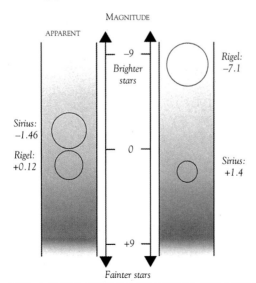

MAGNITUDE

APPARENT

−9
Brighter stars

Rigel:
−7.1

Sirius:
−1.46

Rigel:
+0.12

0

Sirius:
+1.4

+9

Fainter stars

APPARENT VS ABSOLUTE
Sirius is the brightest star in our sky (apparent magnitude −1.46) brighter than Rigel (apparent magnitude +0.12). Yet in reality, Rigel is by far the brighter star with an absolute magnitude of −7.1, as opposed to Sirius which has an absolute magnitude of +1.4.

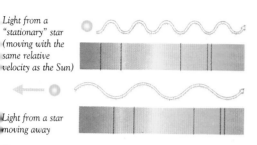

Light from a "stationary" star (moving with the same relative velocity as the Sun)

Light from a star moving away

## BRIGHTNESS FACTS

• With both scales of magnitude, each whole number step (e.g. from +3 to +4) means that the star is $2^1/_2$ times brighter or fainter.

• The Sun's apparent magnitude is –26.7

• The brightest planet is Venus with a maximum apparent magnitude of –4.2.

## SHIFTING LIGHT

All objects in the universe are moving. In light from stars moving away from the Sun, the dark absorption lines are shifted toward the red end of the spectrum – the so-called "red shift."

## HOW FAR?

Calculating a star's absolute magnitude means knowing its distance. For fairly close stars (within a few hundred light-years) astronomers can measure distance using the parallax method. Earth's orbit around the Sun enables astronomers to take two sightings of a star from opposite sides of the orbit. The apparent shift in position of the star between the two sightings is called the parallax. The greater the parallax, the nearer the star. In this case, star A has the greater shift and is the closer.

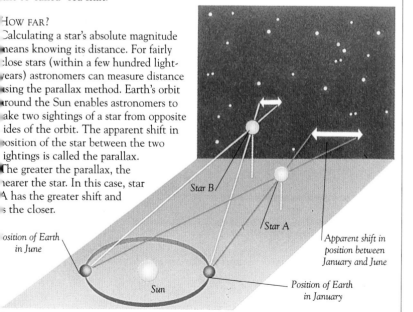

Star B

Star A

Position of Earth in June

Sun

Apparent shift in position between January and June

Position of Earth in January

39

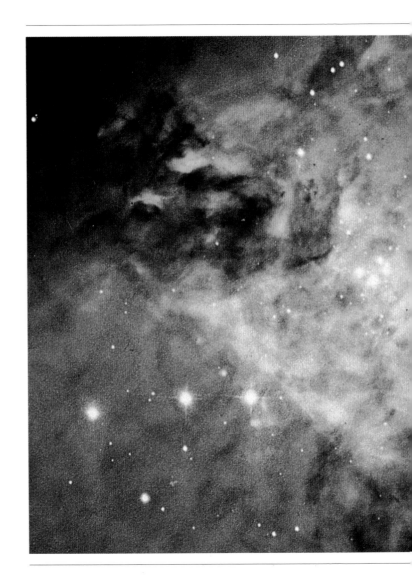

# SPACE FROM EARTH

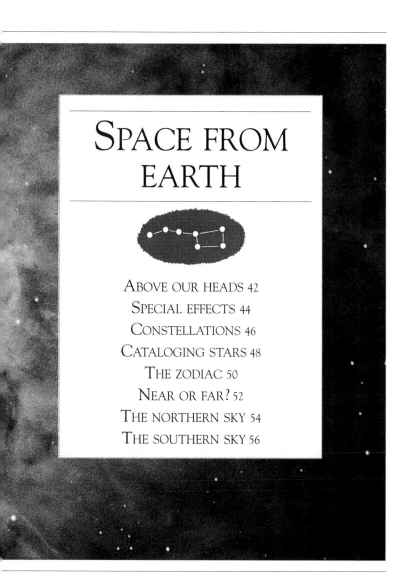

# ABOVE OUR HEADS

OUR KNOWLEDGE of the universe has been gained from our unique position on Earth. By day the sky is dominated by the Sun. At night the blackness of space is studded with stars and galaxies which form an unchanging backdrop. However, our view of them changes throughout the year as Earth orbits the Sun.

CIRCULAR STAR TRAILS
Earth's daily rotation causes the stars to appear to circle around the sky. This effect can be captured by a long-exposure photograph.

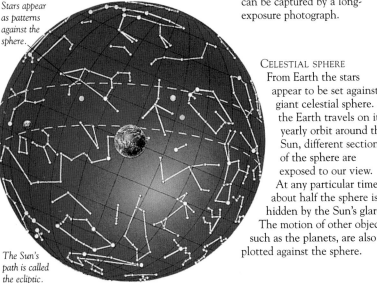

*Stars appear as patterns against the sphere.*

*The Sun's path is called the ecliptic.*

CELESTIAL SPHERE
From Earth the stars appear to be set against a giant celestial sphere. As the Earth travels on its yearly orbit around the Sun, different sections of the sphere are exposed to our view. At any particular time, about half the sphere is hidden by the Sun's glare. The motion of other objects such as the planets, are also plotted against the sphere.

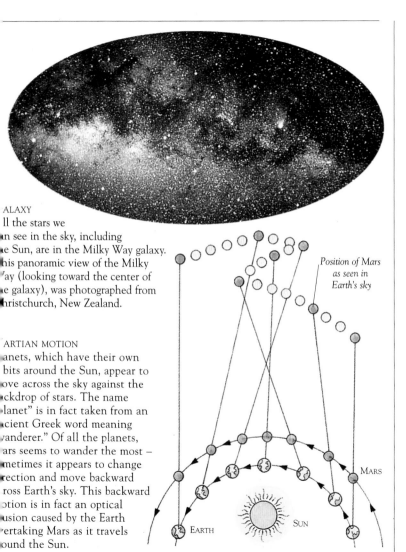

## GALAXY

All the stars we can see in the sky, including the Sun, are in the Milky Way galaxy. This panoramic view of the Milky Way (looking toward the center of the galaxy), was photographed from Christchurch, New Zealand.

## MARTIAN MOTION

Planets, which have their own orbits around the Sun, appear to move across the sky against the backdrop of stars. The name "planet" is in fact taken from an ancient Greek word meaning "wanderer." Of all the planets, Mars seems to wander the most – sometimes it appears to change direction and move backward across Earth's sky. This backward motion is in fact an optical illusion caused by the Earth overtaking Mars as it travels around the Sun.

*Position of Mars as seen in Earth's sky*

MARS

EARTH

SUN

# SPECIAL EFFECTS

FROM EARTH it is possible to see several "special effects" in the sky. Some of these effects are due to peculiarities of the Earth's magnetic field and atmosphere. Other effects depend on the position of the objects in the solar system, especially the Sun, Earth and Moon. Meteor showers are an effect produced by space dust burning up in the atmosphere.

AURORA BOREALIS
Charged particles from the Sun, carried by the solar wind, cause dramatic light shows when they enter Earth's atmosphere.

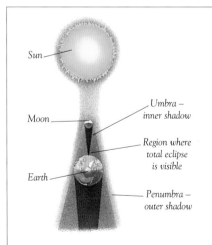

Sun

Moon

Earth

Umbra – inner shadow

Region where total eclipse is visible

Penumbra – outer shadow

ECLIPSE OF THE SUN
Occasionally, the Moon comes into perfect alignment between the Sun and the Earth. When this occurs, the Moon blocks out the Sun's light causing what is called a solar eclipse. From some parts of Earth's surface, the disc of the Moon appears to cover completely the Sun's face, and there is a brief period of darkness. Although the Moon is a great deal smaller than the Sun, it is able to block the light totally because it is so much nearer to the Earth.

## HALO AROUND THE MOON

On some winter nights a halo appears around the Moon, but this has nothing to do with the Moon itself. Sunlight reflected toward Earth by the Moon is refracted (bent) by ice crystals high in Earth's atmosphere. This refraction of light creates a circular halo.

## METEOR RADIANT

Dust particles from space are seen as meteors when they burn up in the atmosphere. In a meteor shower, all the meteors appear to come from a single point in the sky which is called the radiant.

### SPECIAL EFFECT FACTS

• Aurora borealis ("northern lights") are best observed near the north pole. Similar displays in the southern hemisphere are called aurora australis.

• A lunar eclipse occurs when the Earth comes directly between the Sun and the Moon, and the Earth's shadow can be seen crossing the Moon's surface.

• A meteor radiant is an optical illusion. In fact the meteors travel along parallel tracks.

# CONSTELLATIONS

SEEN FROM EARTH, the stars seem to form patterns in the sky. These patterns are known as constellations. The skies around Earth have been divided into 88 different constellations, each one of which is supposed to represent a mythological person, creature, or object.

CONSTELLATION OF ORION
In Greek myth, Orion was a mighty hunter. The three bright stars in a row form Orion's Belt, an easily located "skymark."

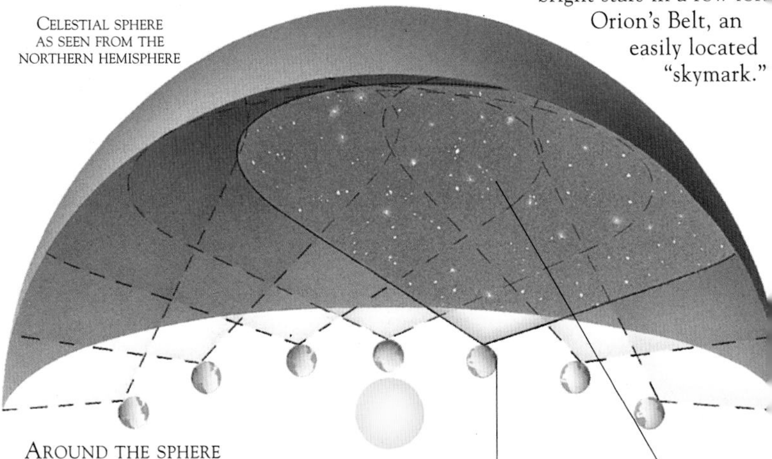

CELESTIAL SPHERE
AS SEEN FROM THE
NORTHERN HEMISPHERE

AROUND THE SPHERE
As the Earth makes its yearly orbit around the Sun, different portions of the celestial sphere come into view, presenting the constellations in an annual sequence.

Position of
Earth
in March

Constellati
visible from I
in Marcl

100,000 YEARS AGO

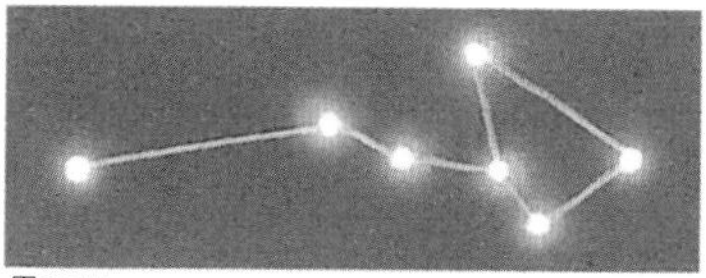

TODAY

100,000 YEARS FROM NOW

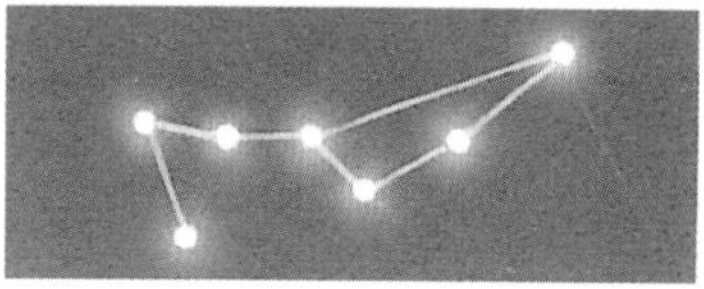

## CHANGING SHAPE

The constellations appear fixed, but in fact they change very slowly. The changes to the Big Dipper can only be seen over very long periods of time.

### CONSTELLATION FACTS

• A constellation is a two-dimensional view of objects in three-dimensional space.

• The Big Dipper (The Plow in the United Kingdom) is not a separate constellation but is part of Ursa Major (the Great Bear).

• Australian aboriginals have their own view of constellations – they see patterns in the dark spaces between stars.

## NES OF SIGHT

he constellations are a
ıman invention. We see them as
at patterns against the blackness
space, but in fact the stars may
farther in distance from each
her than they are from
ırth. The stars in the Big
ipper seem to be close
gether. However,
ey are more
attered than
ey appear.

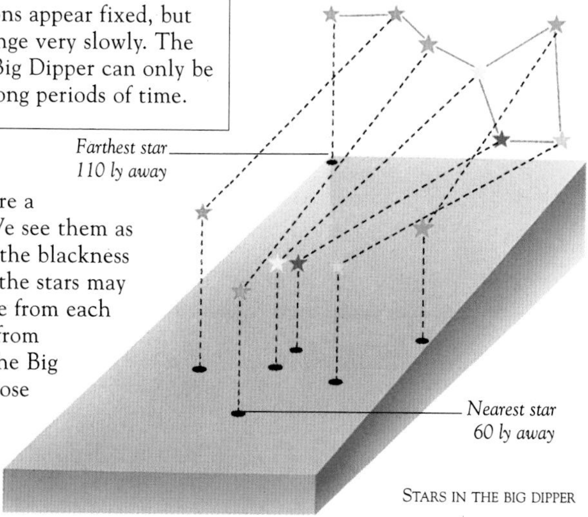

*Farthest star*
*110 ly away*

*Nearest star*
*60 ly away*

STARS IN THE BIG DIPPER

# CATALOGUING STARS

STARS ARE catalogued according to the constellation in which they appear. Within each constellation, the individual stars are identified by means of letters or numbers. Other objects are catalogued separately.

*The constellation "figure" is drawn around the stars.*

ORION

ORION NEBULA
In Earth's sky, the nebula appears as a faint, fuzzy patch of light just below Orion's Belt

POSSESSIVE NAMES
All the constellations have been given Latin names. When referring to a particular star, the possessive case of the Latin name is used. For example, stars in the constellation of Orion are designated Orionis.

MAPPING THE SKIES
The constellations fit together to map the sky. All the stars inside a constellation's boundaries belong to that constellation, even if they appear to be unconnected to the star making up the main "title" figure.

## GALAXIES AND NEBULAE

Nonstellar objects, such as bright star clusters, nebulae, and other galaxies, are classified separately according to the Messier catalogue (numbers prefixed by letter M), or the New General Catalogue (numbers prefixed by the letters NGC).

## GREEK LETTERS

The brighter stars in a constellation are identified by Greek letters. The brightest star is usually designated alpha ($\alpha$), the next brightest beta ($\beta$) and so on, but this rule is not always followed.

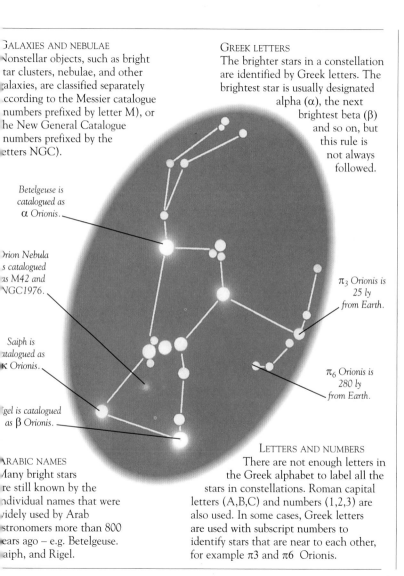

*Betelgeuse is catalogued as $\alpha$ Orionis.*

*Orion Nebula is catalogued as M42 and NGC1976.*

*Saiph is catalogued as $\kappa$ Orionis.*

*Rigel is catalogued as $\beta$ Orionis.*

*$\pi_3$ Orionis is 25 ly from Earth.*

*$\pi_6$ Orionis is 280 ly from Earth.*

## ARABIC NAMES

Many bright stars are still known by the individual names that were widely used by Arab astronomers more than 800 years ago – e.g. Betelgeuse. Saiph, and Rigel.

## LETTERS AND NUMBERS

There are not enough letters in the Greek alphabet to label all the stars in constellations. Roman capital letters (A,B,C) and numbers (1,2,3) are also used. In some cases, Greek letters are used with subscript numbers to identify stars that are near to each other, for example $\pi 3$ and $\pi 6$ Orionis.

# THE ZODIAC

TWELVE CONSTELLATIONS ARE known as the zodiac. These twelve are crossed by the ecliptic (the Sun's annual path around the celestial sphere), and form the backdrop for the movement of the Moon and planets. The Sun spends about a month passing through each zodiac constellation. The dates usually given for the zodiac are approximations – below are the dates when the Sun actually enters each sign.

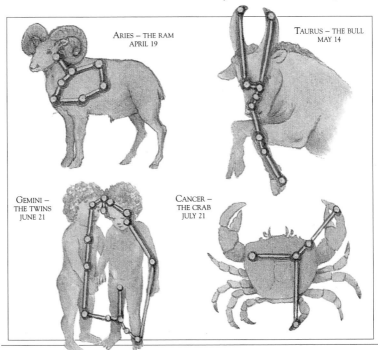

ARIES – THE RAM
APRIL 19

TAURUS – THE BULL
MAY 14

GEMINI –
THE TWINS
JUNE 21

CANCER –
THE CRAB
JULY 21

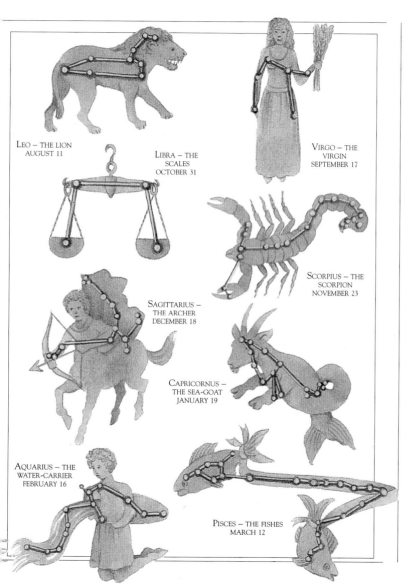

LEO – THE LION
AUGUST 11

LIBRA – THE
SCALES
OCTOBER 31

VIRGO – THE
VIRGIN
SEPTEMBER 17

SCORPIUS – THE
SCORPION
NOVEMBER 23

SAGITTARIUS –
THE ARCHER
DECEMBER 18

CAPRICORNUS –
THE SEA-GOAT
JANUARY 19

AQUARIUS – THE
WATER-CARRIER
FEBRUARY 16

PISCES – THE FISHES
MARCH 12

# NEAR OR FAR?

STARS ARE VAST DISTANCES from us and from each other. Light, which travels faster than anything else, takes 8.3 minutes to travel from the Sun to the Earth. Light from the next nearest star, Proxima Centauri, takes 4.3 years. People cannot tell the distances to stars just by looking at them. But they can see subtle differences in color and apparent brightness.

LIGHT-YEARS APART
All the stars in this distant cluster may look as if they are the same distance from Earth. Yet in fact the stars are many light-years apart.

HOW BRIGHT? HOW FAR?
Stars that have similar apparent magnitude (brightness) can lie at hugely different distances from Earth. Objects in the constellation of Orion are between 70 and 2,300 light-years (ly) from Earth. The brightest star, Rigel, is more than 900 ly away.

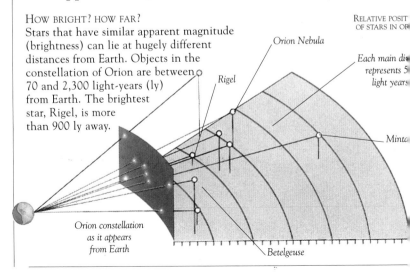

RELATIVE POSIT
OF STARS IN OR

Orion Nebula

Each main div
represents 5
light years

Rigel

Minta

Orion constellation
as it appears
from Earth

Betelgeuse

## STELLAR DATA: NEAREST STARS TO THE SUN

| Name | Distance | Color |
|------|----------|-------|
| Proxima Centauri | 4.2 ly | red |
| α Centauri A | 4.3 ly | yellow |
| α Centauri B | 4.3 ly | orange |
| Barnard's Star | 5.9 ly | red |
| Wolf 359 | 7.6 ly | red |
| Lalande 21185 | 8.1 ly | red |
| Sirius A | 8.6 ly | white |
| Sirius B | 8.6 ly | white |

## STAR FACTS

• Proxima Centauri is part of a triple star system along with α Centauri A and α Centauri B.

• The brightest star, Sirius A, has a faint white dwarf companion, Sirius B.

## NEIGHBORING STARS

Many of the stars within 40 light-years of the Sun are dim red dwarfs like Barnard's Star, which cannot be seen with the naked eye. Others, such as Vega, are 50 times more luminous than the Sun.

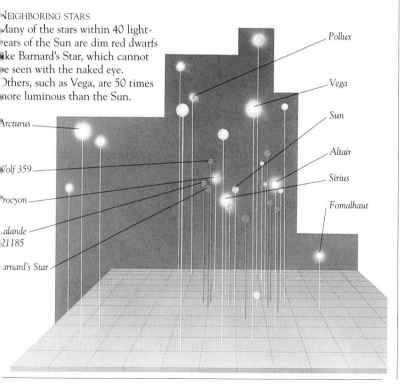

Pollux

Vega

Sun

Altair

Sirius

Fomalhaut

Arcturus

Wolf 359

Procyon

Lalande 21185

Barnard's Star

# THE NORTHERN SKY

PEOPLE LIVING IN the Northern Hemisphere see the northern half of the celestial sphere. The stars visible on a particular night depend on the observer's latitude, the time of year, and the time of night. The stars near the center of the sky-map are called circumpolar and can be seen throughout the year. Polaris (the North Star) appears to remain directly over the North Pole.

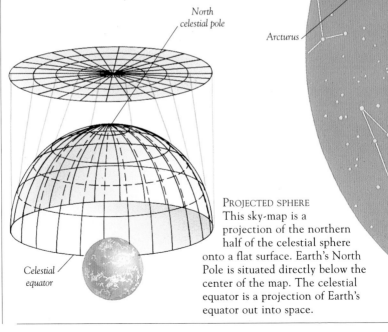

*North celestial pole*

*Arcturus*

*Celestial equator*

PROJECTED SPHERE
This sky-map is a projection of the northern half of the celestial sphere onto a flat surface. Earth's North Pole is situated directly below the center of the map. The celestial equator is a projection of Earth's equator out into space.

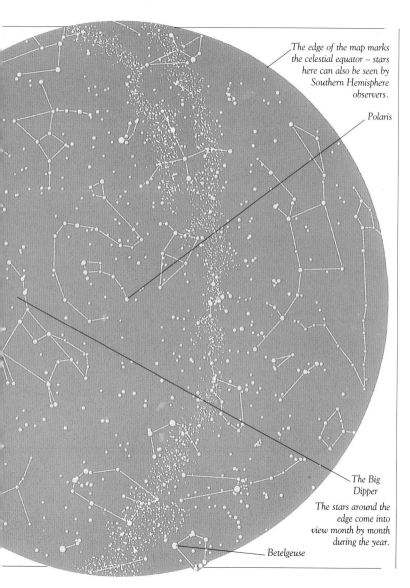

The edge of the map marks the celestial equator – stars here can also be seen by Southern Hemisphere observers.

Polaris

The Big Dipper

The stars around the edge come into view month by month during the year.

Betelgeuse

# THE SOUTHERN SKY

PEOPLE LIVING IN the Southern Hemisphere see the
southern half of the celestial sphere. The stars
visible on a particular night depend on the
observer's latitude, the time of year, and
the time of night. The stars near the center
of the sky-map are called circumpolar
and can be seen all year round. Alpha
Centauri, one of the nearest stars to the
Sun, is a southern hemisphere star.

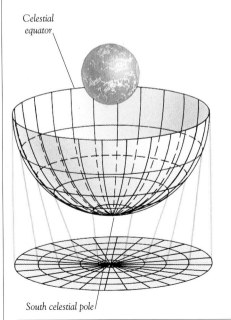

*Celestial equator*

*Alpha Centauri*

*Antares*

*South celestial pole*

PROJECTED SPHERE
This sky-map is a
projection of the
southern half of the
celestial sphere onto a
flat surface. Earth's South
Pole is situated directly
below the center of the
map. The celestial equator
is a projection of Earth's
equator out into space.

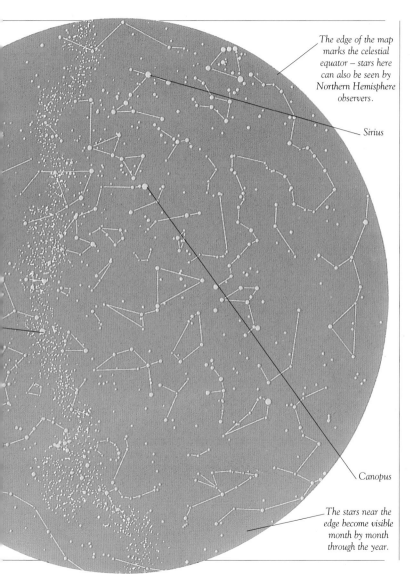

The edge of the map
marks the celestial
equator – stars here
can also be seen by
Northern Hemisphere
observers.

Sirius

Canopus

The stars near the
edge become visible
month by month
through the year.

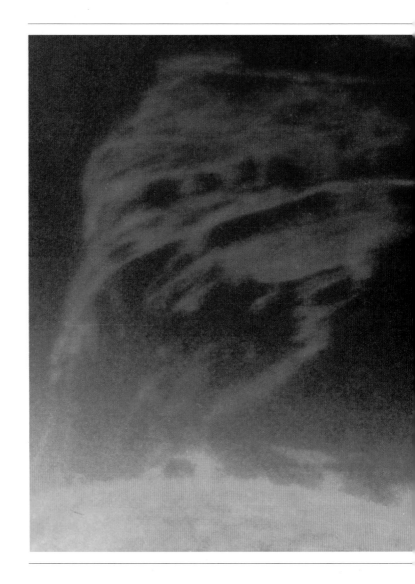

# SOLAR SYSTEM

# WHAT IS THE SOLAR SYSTEM?

THE SOLAR SYSTEM consists of the Sun and the many objects that orbit around it – nine planets, over 60 moons, and countless asteroids and comets. The system occupies a disk-shaped volume of space more than 7.45 billion miles (12 billion kilometers) across. At the center is the Sun which contains more than 99 percent of the solar system's mass.

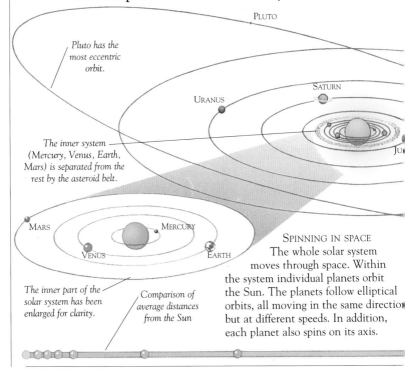

PLUTO

*Pluto has the most eccentric orbit.*

SATURN

URANUS

*The inner system (Mercury, Venus, Earth, Mars) is separated from the rest by the asteroid belt.*

JU

MARS

MERCURY

VENUS

EARTH

*The inner part of the solar system has been enlarged for clarity.*

*Comparison of average distances from the Sun*

SPINNING IN SPACE
The whole solar system moves through space. Within the system individual planets orbit the Sun. The planets follow elliptical orbits, all moving in the same direction but at different speeds. In addition, each planet also spins on its axis.

## SOLAR SYSTEM FACTS

• Images obtained with the latest telescopes strongly suggest that some other stars (e.g. β Pictoris) are forming planetary systems.

• The solar system has a total of 61 moons by the latest count. Future space probes are almost certain to discover extra moons orbiting the outer planets.

MERCURY

VENUS

EARTH

MARS

*Each of the four gas planets has a ring system around it – the rings have been omitted from this illustration for ease of comparison.*

JUPITER

*Orbits are elliptical (oval) rather than circular*

NEPTUNE

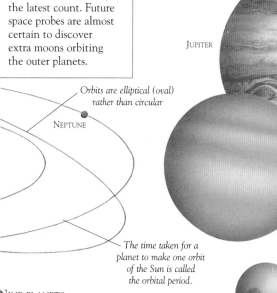

SATURN

*The time taken for a planet to make one orbit of the Sun is called the orbital period.*

URANUS

NEPTUNE

## NINE PLANETS

The planets form two main groups – the inner four are composed of rock, while the next four are larger and are composed mostly of liquefied gas. The outermost planet, Pluto, is mainly rock.

PLUTO

*Pluto is the smallest and least-known planet.*

# SOLAR GRAVITY

ABOUT 4.6 BILLION years ago, the solar system formed from a cloud of gas and dust. The Sun formed first and the other objects formed from the leftovers. The Sun's gravity dominates the system because it is so massive by comparison with the planets.

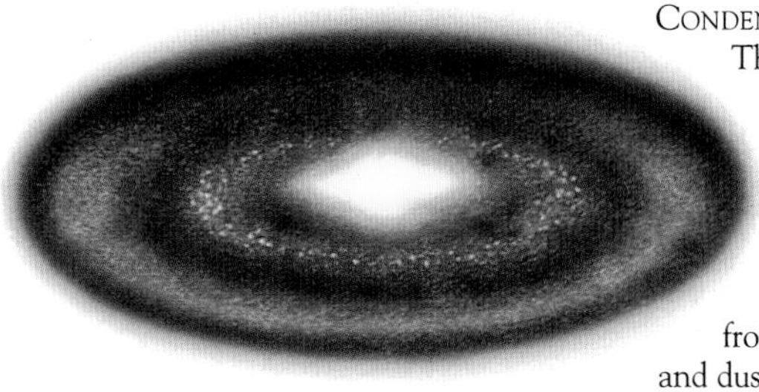

CONDENSING INTO PLACE
The young Sun was surrounded by a cloud of gas, snow, and dust that flattened into a disk. Dust clumped together to form the four inner rock planets. The giant outer planets formed from a mixture of gas, snow, and dust. Pluto's origin is a mystery.

ORBITAL PATHS
Most of the planets orbit close to the plane of the Earth's orbit (the ecliptic). Pluto has the most inclined orbit, possibly because it is the most distant planet and is the least influenced by the Sun's gravity. However the next most inclined planet is Mercury (7°), which is the nearest planet to the Sun.

THE PLANETS:
ORBITAL INCLINATION
TO THE ECLIPTIC

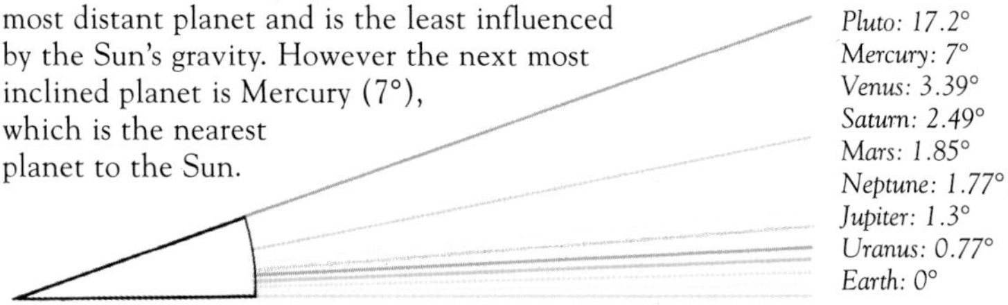

Pluto: 17.2°
Mercury: 7°
Venus: 3.39°
Saturn: 2.49°
Mars: 1.85°
Neptune: 1.77°
Jupiter: 1.3°
Uranus: 0.77°
Earth: 0°

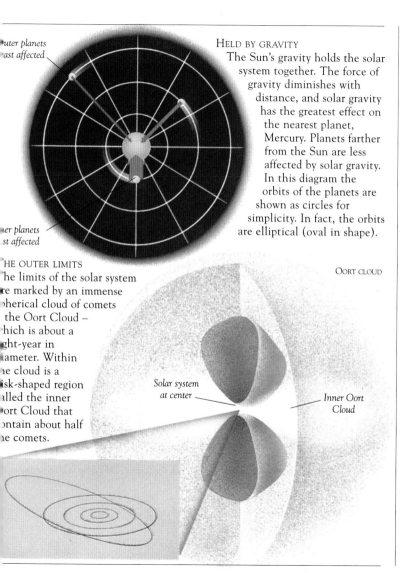

**Outer planets
least affected**

## HELD BY GRAVITY

The Sun's gravity holds the solar
system together. The force of
gravity diminishes with
distance, and solar gravity
has the greatest effect on
the nearest planet,
Mercury. Planets farther
from the Sun are less
affected by solar gravity.
In this diagram the
orbits of the planets are
shown as circles for
simplicity. In fact, the orbits
are elliptical (oval in shape).

**Inner planets
most affected**

## THE OUTER LIMITS

The limits of the solar system
are marked by an immense
spherical cloud of comets
the Oort Cloud –
which is about a
light-year in
diameter. Within
the cloud is a
disk-shaped region
called the inner
Oort Cloud that
contain about half
the comets.

OORT CLOUD

*Solar system
at center*

*Inner Oort
Cloud*

# THE SUN

LIKE OTHER STARS, the Sun is a huge ball of spinning gas. Nuclear reactions take place at its core, giving off energy. The Sun is the only star close enough to be studied in detail. Its surface features, such as sunspots and prominences, can be observed from Earth. Satellites and space probes are able to get a closer view and obtain even more information.

ECLIPSE OF THE SUN
During an eclipse, the outer layer of the Sun, the corona, becomes visible. Normally the corona is hidden by glare.

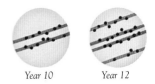

Year 1    Year 4    Year 7    Year 10    Year 12

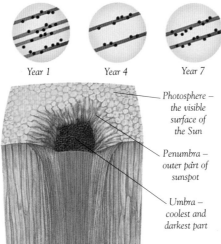

Photosphere – the visible surface of the Sun

Penumbra – outer part of sunspot

Umbra – coolest and darkest part

COOL AND DARK
Sunspots, dark patches on the surface, are regions of cooler gas caused by disturbances in the Sun's magnetic field. Sunspots follow an 11-year cycle that begins with the Sun being spot-free. The spots appear at high latitude and gradually increase in number, moving toward the Sun's equator during the cycle.

## SOLAR DATA

| | |
|---|---|
| Average distance from Earth | 93,026,724 miles (149,680,000 km) |
| Distance from center of galaxy | 30,000 light-years |
| Diameter (at equator) | 865,121 miles (1,391,980 km) |
| Rotation period (at equator) | 25.04 Earth days |
| Mass (Earth = 1) | 330,000 |
| Gravity (Earth = 1) | 27.9 |
| Average density (water = 1) | 1.41 |
| Absolute magnitude | 4.83 |

## SOLAR FACTS

• **Never look directly at the Sun. Even with sunglasses, camera film, or smoked glass you risk damaging your eyesight.**

• The safe way is to project the Sun's image onto a piece of paper using a hand lens.

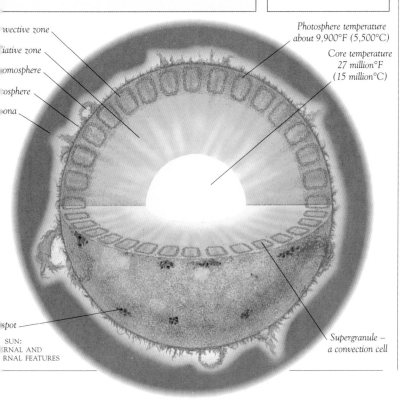

*wective zone*

*iative zone*

*omosphere*

*:osphere*

*ona*

*Photosphere temperature about 9,900°F (5,500°C)*

*Core temperature 27 million°F (15 million°C)*

*spot*

SUN:
RNAL AND
RNAL FEATURES

*Supergranule – a convection cell*

65

# SOLAR ENERGY AND INFLUENCE

AT ITS CORE, the Sun converts hydrogen to helium at a
rate of 600 million tons (tonnes)
every second. The energy
produced eventually
reaches the surface and
travels through space.

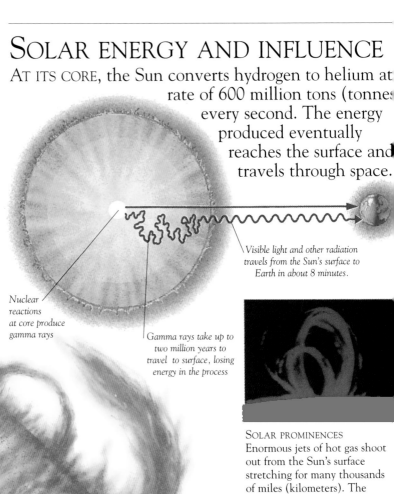

*Visible light and other radiation
travels from the Sun's surface to
Earth in about 8 minutes.*

Nuclear
reactions
at core produce
gamma rays

Gamma rays take up to
two million years to
travel to surface, losing
energy in the process

SOLAR PROMINENCES
Enormous jets of hot gas shoot
out from the Sun's surface
stretching for many thousands
of miles (kilometers). The
largest jets, called prominences,
can last for several months. The
Sun's magnetic field holds some
prominences in gigantic loops.

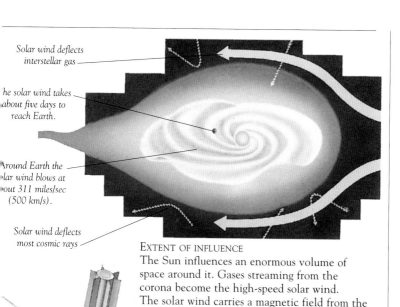

*Solar wind deflects interstellar gas*

*The solar wind takes about five days to reach Earth.*

*Around Earth the solar wind blows at about 311 miles/sec (500 km/s).*

*Solar wind deflects most cosmic rays*

ULYSSES
SOLAR PROBE

*Sensors located on hinged boom*

## EXTENT OF INFLUENCE

The Sun influences an enormous volume of space around it. Gases streaming from the corona become the high-speed solar wind. The solar wind carries a magnetic field from the Sun. As the Sun rotates, the field takes on a spiral shape. The volume of space swept by the solar wind is called the heliosphere.

## TO THE SOLAR POLES

Earth's orbit in the Sun's equatorial plane means that the Sun's poles cannot be studied from Earth. The Ulysses probe was launched in 1990 to study these hard-to-observe regions.

---

### SOLAR ENERGY FACTS

• Converting hydrogen to helium means that the Sun loses four million tons (tonnes) of its mass every second.

• The amount of the Sun's energy reaching Earth's atmosphere (known as the solar constant) is equivalent to 1.37 kw (kilowatts) of electricity per square meter.

# PLANETS

# MERCURY

A SMALL ROCK WORLD with a large dense core, Mercury is the closest planet to the Sun. There is no real atmosphere, and much of the surface is marked by numerous impact craters. Dominated by the Sun, Mercury experiences the greatest variation in surface temperature of any planet in the solar system. Differences between day and night can be more than 1,080°F (600°C).

DIFFICULT TO SEE
Photographs taken from Earth show Mercury as a fuzzy disk, difficult to observe against the Sun. This image was put together from photographs taken by the Mariner 10 probe.

*Earth*

*Mercury*

MERCURY: PLANETARY DATA

| | |
|---|---|
| Average distance from the Sun | 36 million miles (57.9 million km) |
| Orbital period | 88 Earth days |
| Orbital velocity | 29.7 miles/sec (47.9 km/s) |
| Rotation period | 58.7 Earth days |
| Diameter at equator | 3,032 miles (4,878 km) |
| Surface temperature | −292°F to +806°F (−180°C to +430°C) |
| Mass (Earth = 1) | 0.055 |
| Gravity (Earth = 1) | 0.38 |
| Number of moons | 0 |

MERCURY FACTS

• Mercury was named after the fleet-footed messenger of the Roman gods because it travels so quickly across Earth's sky.

• Mercury's largest crater, Caloris Planitia, measures 875 miles (1,400 km) across.

56% oxygen

35% sodium

8% helium

1% potassium and hydrogen

MERCURY:
COMPOSITION OF ATMOSPHERE

## THIN AIR

Mercury's atmosphere is extremely thin – less than one trillionth of Earth's. Sodium and potassium occur in the daytime only, as the Sun's energy releases them from the planet's surface.

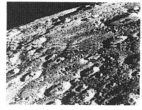

PROBE'S EYE VIEW
Craters cover about 60 percent of Mercury's surface. The other 40 percent consists of relatively smooth plains.

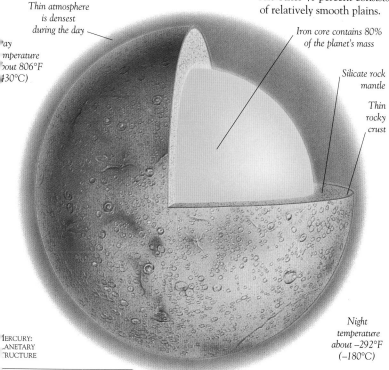

Thin atmosphere is densest during the day

Day temperature about 806°F (430°C)

Iron core contains 80% of the planet's mass

Silicate rock mantle

Thin rocky crust

Night temperature about –292°F (–180°C)

MERCURY:
PLANETARY
STRUCTURE

71

## LONG DAYS

Mercury rotates very slowly on an almost upright axis. The axis is tilted at just 2° from the normal (at 90°) to the plane of its orbit. A single day on Mercury (sunrise to sunrise) lasts for 176 Earth days. Although days are very long, the Mercurian year is very short. The planet takes only 88 Earth days to complete one orbit around the Sun.

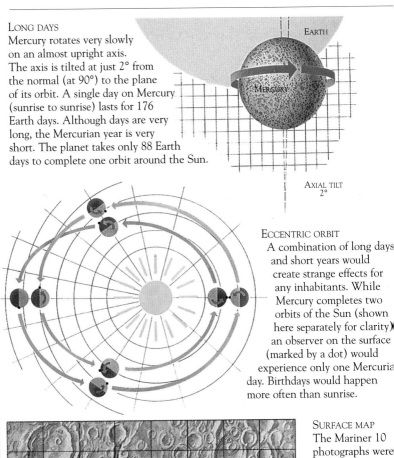

EARTH

MERCURY

AXIAL TILT
2°

## ECCENTRIC ORBIT

A combination of long days and short years would create strange effects for any inhabitants. While Mercury completes two orbits of the Sun (shown here separately for clarity) an observer on the surface (marked by a dot) would experience only one Mercurial day. Birthdays would happen more often than sunrise.

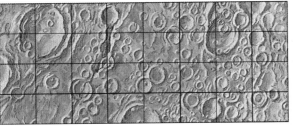

## SURFACE MAP

The Mariner 10 photographs were used to produce maps of Mercury. Each square of the grid covers about 50 x 50 miles (80 x 80 km).

## IMPACT CRATER FORMATION ON ROCK PLANETS

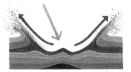

A meteorite impact blasts out a circular crater, and ejected material falls back to form a circular rim.

Rock compressed by the initial impact may bounce back from the sides to form a roughly conical central peak.

The crater profile is gradually reduced as rock fragments and debris slip from the walls and peak.

## SOLITARY VISITOR

Mariner 10 is the only probe to have made a detailed study of Mercury. Launched in November 1973, the probe took five months to reach the planet. During three close approaches the probe photographed about 40 percent of the surface area. At its closest approach, Mariner 10 was 187 miles (300 km) above the surface.

*High resolution cameras*

MARINER 10 PROBE

## MERCURY: CREATIVE CRATER NAMES

Mercury's craters commemorate creative people:

| Writers | Composers | Painters | Architects |
|---------|-----------|----------|------------|
| Bronte | Bach | Brueghel | Bernini |
| Cervantes | Chopin | Cezanne | Bramante |
| Dickens | Grieg | Dürer | Imhotep |
| Goethe | Handel | Holbein | Mansart |
| Li Po | Liszt | Monet | Michelangelo |
| Melville | Mozart | Renoir | Sinan |
| Shelley | Stravinsky | Titian | Sullivan |
| Tolstoy | Verdi | Van Gogh | Wren |

## FACTS

• Mercury can only be seen from Earth at twilight – either just before dawn or just after sunset.

• Parts of Mercury's surface have a wrinkled appearance – the result of the planet shrinking as its core cooled.

# VENUS

A ROCK PLANET with a dense atmosphere, Venus is almost the same size as the Earth. The two share some surface features, but conditions on Venus are very different from those on Earth. The surface environment of Venus is extremely hostile – intense heat, crushing pressure, and unbreathable air. Overhead there are thick clouds of sulfuric acid droplets.

OBSCURED BY CLOUDS
The surface features of Venus are hidden by a permanent blanket of thick cloud. The dark swirls are high-altitude wind systems.

*Venus*

*Earth*

| VENUS: PLANETARY DATA | |
| --- | --- |
| Average distance from the Sun | 67.2 million miles (108.2 million km) |
| Orbital period | 224.7 Earth days |
| Orbital velocity | 21.7 miles/sec (35 km/s) |
| Rotation period | 243 Earth days |
| Diameter at equator | 7,521 miles (12,102 km) |
| Surface temperature | 896°F (480°C) |
| Mass (Earth = 1) | 0.81 |
| Gravity (Earth = 1) | 0.88 |
| Number of moons | 0 |

VENUS FACTS

• Venus shines brightly in Earth's sky because the cloud layer reflects most of the sunlight.

• Venus has phases like the Moon. You need a telescope to see them clearly, but binoculars will enable you to see the crescent phase.

*Upper haze*

*Cloud layer 12.5 miles (20 km) thick*

*Lower haze*

0.5% *sulfur dioxide, argon, and carbon monoxide*

BENEATH THE CLOUDS
Below the clouds is a clear carbon-dioxide atmosphere. At the surface, atmospheric pressure is 90 times that of Earth at sea level.

| 96% carbon dioxide |

3.5% *nitrogen*

0.5% *sulphur dioxide, argon, and carbon monoxide*

COMPUTER IMAGE
This is a computer-generated image of the Howe meteorite crater 23 miles (37 km) in diameter. The image was produced from radar-mapping data.

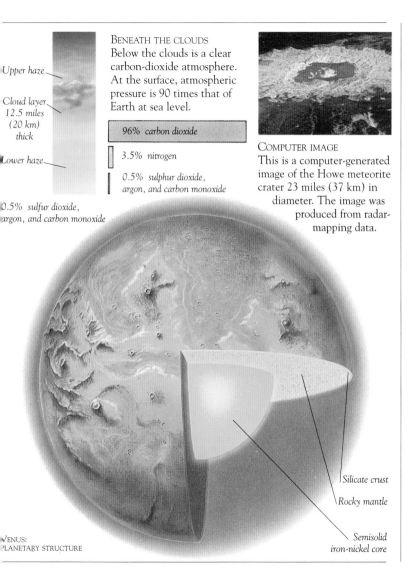

*Silicate crust*

*Rocky mantle*

*Semisolid iron-nickel core*

VENUS:
PLANETARY STRUCTURE

### BACKWARD ROTATION

Venus is one of only two planets to rotate on its axis in a backward direction (the other is remote Pluto). Venus' backward rotation is so slow that a Venusian day lasts longer (243 Earth days) than a Venusian year (224.7 Earth days). Driven by powerful winds, Venus' atmosphere moves at its own, much faster, pace. The upper levels of the cloud layer take just four Earth days to travel right around the planet.

AXIAL TILT
2°

EARTH

VENUS

62 miles
(100 km)

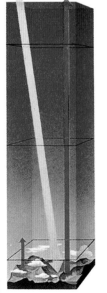

EARTH

VENUS

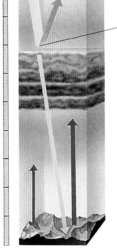

Sunlight reflected
by cloud layer

### GREENHOUSE PLANET

Venus has a higher average surface temperature (896°F -480°C ) than any other planet in the solar system. The heating of Venus is the result of a "greenhouse effect" run wild. Although the cloud layer reflects much of the sunlight that hits it, some solar heat energy does reach the surface. But instead of being radiated back into space, the heat energy is trapped by the cloud layer causing temperatures to rise. On Earth the cloud layer allows much more heat to escape.

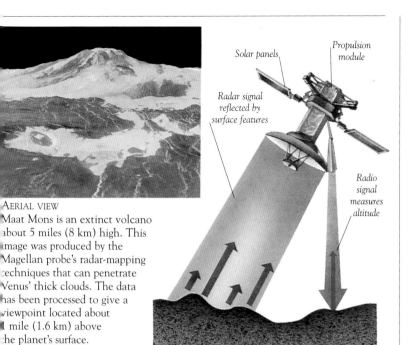

Solar panels

Propulsion module

Radar signal reflected by surface features

Radio signal measures altitude

AERIAL VIEW
Maat Mons is an extinct volcano about 5 miles (8 km) high. This image was produced by the Magellan probe's radar-mapping techniques that can penetrate Venus' thick clouds. The data has been processed to give a viewpoint located about 1 mile (1.6 km) above the planet's surface.

| Probe | Date | Result |
|---|---|---|
| Mariner 2 | 14/12/62 | Successful flyby |
| Venera 4 | 18/10/67 | Sampled atmosphere |
| Venera 7 | 15/12/70 | Sent data from surface |
| Mariner 10 | 5/2/74 | Flyby on way to Mercury |
| Venera 9 | 23/10/75 | First orbit and soft landing and first surface image |
| Venera 15 | 10/10/83 | First radar mapping |
| Pioneer-Venus 2 | 9/12/78 | Multiple descent probes investigate atmosphere |
| Magellan | 10/8/90 | Complete radar mapping |

VENUS: SELECTED EXPLORATION EVENTS

MORE FACTS
• The facts that Venus has a small axial tilt and backward rotation is just popular convention. According to the rules of the IAU (International Astronomical Union), Venus rotates in a normal direction around an axis tilted at 177.9° to the vertical.

# EARTH

THE THIRD PLANET from the Sun, Earth, is unique in the solar system and is possibly unique in the universe. Only Earth has the surface conditions that permit liquid water to exist, and Earth alone has developed an oxygen-rich atmosphere. These two factors have enabled the rocky planet Earth to evolve myriad varieties of life.

JEWEL IN SPACE
Photographed by Apollo astronauts returning from the Moon, planet Earth looks like a brightly colored jewel – blue oceans, white clouds, and green-brown land masses.

*Earth*

| EARTH: PLANETARY DATA | |
| --- | --- |
| Average distance from the Sun | 93 million miles (149.6 million km) |
| Orbital period | 365.25 days |
| Orbital velocity | 18.5 miles/sec (29.8 km/s) |
| Rotation period | 23.93 hours |
| Diameter at equator | 7,928 miles (12,756 km) |
| Surface temperature | –94°F to +131°F (–70°C to +55°C) |
| Gravity (Earth = 1) | 1 |
| Number of moons | 1 |

EARTH FACTS
• The oldest rocks so far discovered in the Earth's crust date back 3.9 billion years.

• The oxygen in Earth's atmosphere is the result of life. The process of oxygenation began with bacteria about 2 billion years ago.

Meteoroids
burn up

zone layer

Clouds of
water vapor

RTH: ATMOSPHERE
UCTURE AND COMPOSITION

ust of
ate rock

stly solid
ate mantle

lten
er core

ARTH:
ANETARY STRUCTURE

## ATMOSPHERIC ENGINE
Earth's atmosphere acts like a
huge solar-powered engine,
transporting and redistributing
water around the planet as
clouds and rain.

| 78% nitrogen |
| :-- |

21% oxygen

1% water vapor, carbon
dioxide, and trace gases

## WATER AT WORK
A satellite view of the
Ganges Delta, Bangladesh,
shows natural processes at
work. As well as carrying
rainwater from distant
mountains, the
river also carries
sediment to
the sea.

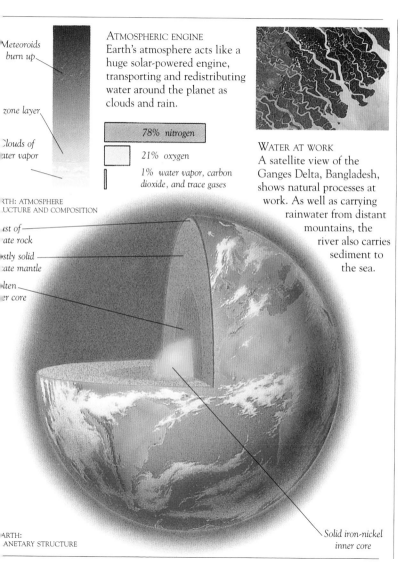

Solid iron-nickel
inner core

## UNEQUAL HEATING

Earth's axis of rotation is tilted at 23.5° to the vertical. As the planet travels around the Sun during the year, the tilt causes seasonal variations in climate. These variations are most noticeable in the high latitudes away from the equator. Spinning on a tilted axis gives rise to unequal heating of the surface by the Sun. This differential heating produces differences in atmospheric pressure which create the wind systems that drive Earth's climate.

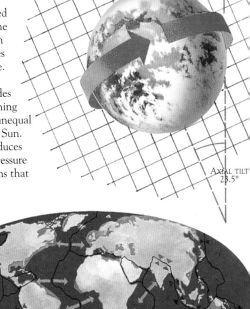

AXIAL TILT
23.5°

200 MYA

60 MYA

### 200 MILLION YEARS AGO
The continents were grouped closer together.

### 60 MILLION YEARS AGO
The landmasses had moved some way toward their present locations.

## CONTINENTS IN MOTION

The continents "float" on the surface of the Earth's crust, which is made up of a number of separate plates. These plates are in constant slow-motion, pushed apart as new crust is produced at mid-ocean ridges. The result is that the continents are also gradually moving. Areas where plates are in collision have many volcanoes and earthquakes.

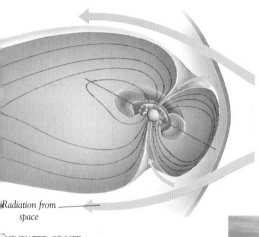

Radiation from space

SPINNING MAGNET

Earth has a much stronger magnetic field than any of the other rock planets. Produced by the rapid rotation of the nickel-iron core, the magnetic field extends far into space and deflects harmful radiation away from the planet. Despite its elongated ovoid shape, this magnetic field is called the magnetosphere.

THE WATER OF LIFE

Water only exists in its liquid form between 2°F (0°C) and 212°F (100°C), which is about the same range of temperatures found on Earth. Liquid water is absolutely essential to practically all forms of life. Along with carbon dioxide, it is one of the two raw materials used by plants to produce their own food and provide the oxygen upon which animal life depends.

| EARTH: PHYSICAL LIMITS | |
| --- | --- |
| Age | 4.6 billion years |
| Mass | 59,760 trillion tons (tonnes) |
| Surface area | 317 million sq miles |
| | (510 million km²) |
| Covered by water | 70.8 percent |
| Highest mountain | 29,028 ft (8,848 meters) |
| Deepest ocean trench | 35,800 ft (10,924 meters) |
| Oldest evidence of life | 3.5 billion years ago |
| Total number of living species | at least 10 million |

MORE FACTS

• The Atlantic Ocean increases in width by about 1.2 in (3 cm) each year.

• Earth has periodic magnetic reversals when the north pole becomes the south pole, and the south becomes north.

# EARTH'S MOON

EARTH HAS A single satellite, the Moon, which is about one-quarter the size of our planet. Although the Earth and the Moon are closely linked, there are many striking contrasts. The Moon is a waterless, airless, and lifeless place. Its surface is covered by craters, the scars of a massive meteorite bombardment that took place billions of years ago.

FAMILIAR SIGHT
Some of the features on the Moon can be identified with the naked eye. Binoculars, or a small telescope, will reveal a considerable amount of detail.

 *The Moon's distance from Earth varies during its orbit.*

Minimum    Average    Maximum

| THE MOON: DATA | |
| --- | --- |
| Average distance from the Earth | 238,970 miles (384,500 km) |
| Orbital period | 27.3 Earth days |
| Orbital velocity | 0.6 miles/sec (1 km/s ) |
| Rotation period | 27.3 Earth days |
| Diameter at equator | 2,160 miles (3,476 km) |
| Surface temperature | −247°F to +221°F (−155°C to +105°C) |
| Mass (Earth = 1) | 0.012 |
| Gravity (Earth = 1) | 0.16 |
| Escape velocity | 1.48 miles/sec (2.38 km/s) |

MOON FACTS
• The Moon has approximately the same surface area as the continents of North and South America.

• The pull of the Moon's gravity is largely responsible for the twice daily rise and fall of tides in Earth's seas and oceans.

### FIGURE IN A MOONSCAPE

The Moon remains unique as the only extraterrestrial object upon which human beings have walked. Protected by a spacesuit from the airless lunar environment, one of the Apollo 17 astronauts investigates a large boulder. Undisturbed by the effects of wind or rain, his footprints should remain visible for millions of years.

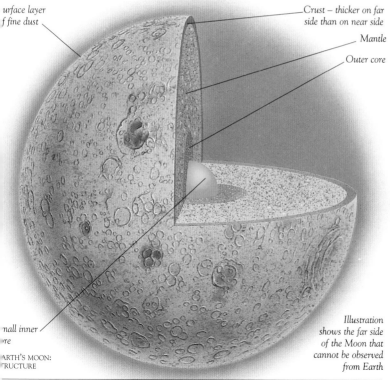

Surface layer of fine dust

Crust – thicker on far side than on near side

Mantle

Outer core

Small inner core

EARTH'S MOON: STRUCTURE

*Illustration shows the far side of the Moon that cannot be observed from Earth*

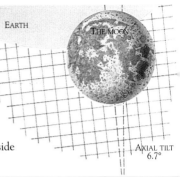
EARTH

THE MOON

AXIAL TILT 6.7°

HELD IN PLACE

Earth is larger and more massive than the Moon, and has a powerful effect on its smaller neighbor. Under the influence of Earth's gravity the Moon's motion through space has been moderated so that its rotation period is the same as its orbital period – 27.3 days. This synchronization of motion means that the same face of the Moon is always turned toward the Earth – the near side. The other side is always turned away from us – the far side.

BATTERED SURFACE

About 3.8 billion years ago, the Moon's surface received an intense meteorite bombardment.

Some 1 billion years later, the largest craters gradually filled up with dark lava, and formed the lunar seas.

Since that time, the appearance of the lunar surface has hardly changed apart from a few recent ray craters.

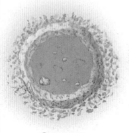

OLD CRATER

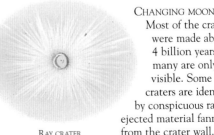

RAY CRATER

CHANGING MOONSCAPE

Most of the craters were made about 4 billion years ago, and many are only faintly visible. Some newer craters are identifiable by conspicuous rays of pale ejected material fanning out from the crater wall.

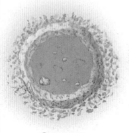

PLANETS

## MOON ROCK

About 836 lb (380 kg) of moon rock have been brought
back to Earth. There are no sedimentary or metamorphic
rocks on the Moon – all the samples brought
back are either igneous lavas
(mainly basalt) or breccias
produced by the heat
and force of meteorite
impacts. Most of the
Moon's surface is
covered with a layer of
crushed and broken rock
(called "regolith") which
is about 65 ft (20 m) deep.

MOON ROCK COLLECTED
BY APOLLO ASTRONAUTS

PHASES OF THE MOON

*Waning*

*Full Moon*

SUNLIGHT

New Moon

*Waxing*

The Moon shines by reflected
sunlight. As it travels around
the Earth, the visible
amount of sunlit area
changes day by day.
Viewed from Earth's
surface, this produces a
cycle of lunar phases –
waxing from New Moon to
Full Moon, and then waning
back to New Moon once more.

## EARTH'S MOON: SELECTED EXPLORATION EVENTS

| Vehicle | Date | Result |
|---------|------|--------|
| Luna 3 | 10/10/59 | First images of far side |
| Luna 9 | 3/2/66 | First soft landing |
| Surveyor 3 | 17/4/67 | Landing site soil studies |
| Apollo 11 | 20/7/69 | Humans first land on Moon |
| Luna 16 | 24/9/70 | Robot returns with samples |
| Luna 17 | 17/11/70 | Mobile robot landed |
| Apollo 15 | 30/7/71 | Lunar Roving Vehicle used |
| Apollo 17 | 11/12/72 | Last Apollo mission lands |

### MORE FACTS

• The first person to
step on to the Moon
was the astronaut Neil
Armstrong early on
July 21, 1969.

• His historic first
words were, " That's
one small step for a
man, one giant leap
for mankind."

# MARS

A RED-HUED ROCKY PLANET, Mars is a cold, barren world with a thin atmosphere. There are many Earthlike features, such as polar ice caps and water-carved valleys, but there are many important differences. Temperatures rarely rise above the freezing point, the air is unbreathable, and dust-storms occasionally scour the surface. The planet's red color is caused by the presence of iron oxide.

LONG RANGE VIEW
This image was obtained by an Earth-orbiting telescope at a distance of 53 million miles (85 million km) from Mars. Bluish clouds can be seen above the north pole region.

*Earth*

*Mars*

| MARS: PLANETARY DATA | |
| --- | --- |
| Average distance from the Sun | 141.6 million miles (227.9 million km) |
| Orbital period | 687 Earth days |
| Orbital velocity | 15 miles/sec (24.1 km/s) |
| Rotation period | 24.62 hours |
| Diameter at equator | 4,217 miles (6,786 km) |
| Surface temperature | −184°F to +77°F (−120°C to +25°C) |
| Mass (Earth = 1) | 0.107 |
| Gravity (Earth = 1) | 0.38 |
| Moons: | 2 |

MARS FACTS

• Mars was named after the Roman god of war because it appears the color of spilled blood.

• The south polar ice cap on Mars is much larger than the north polar ice cap, and the southern winter is considerably longer.

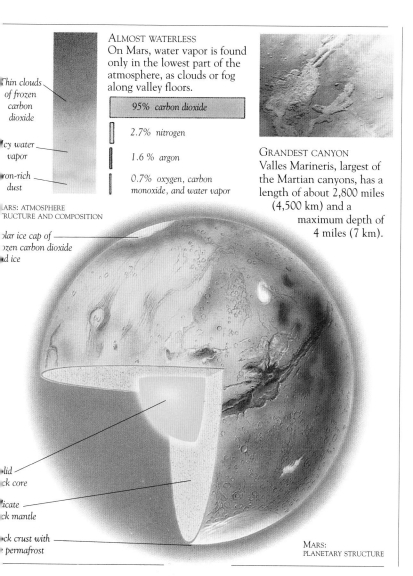

### ALMOST WATERLESS
On Mars, water vapor is found only in the lowest part of the atmosphere, as clouds or fog along valley floors.

| 95% carbon dioxide |
|---|

2.7% nitrogen

1.6 % argon

0.7% oxygen, carbon monoxide, and water vapor

Thin clouds of frozen carbon dioxide

Icy water vapor

Iron-rich dust

MARS: ATMOSPHERE
STRUCTURE AND COMPOSITION

### GRANDEST CANYON
Valles Marineris, largest of the Martian canyons, has a length of about 2,800 miles (4,500 km) and a maximum depth of 4 miles (7 km).

Polar ice cap of frozen carbon dioxide and ice

Solid rock core

Silicate rock mantle

Rock crust with permafrost

MARS:
PLANETARY STRUCTURE

### EARTHLIKE SEASONS

Mars is smaller than the Earth, but turns on its axis more slowly, so that the day lengths are almost identical. A day on Mars is just 41 minutes longer. A similar axial tilt gives Mars the same pattern of seasons as we experience on Earth. However, because of the greater orbital period (687 Earth days), the length of each season is nearly twice as long.

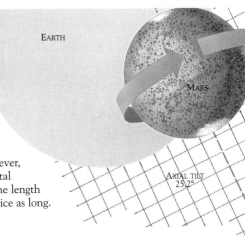

EARTH

MARS

AXIAL TILT
25.2°

### DESERT SURFACE

This is a view of the Martian surface photographed by the Viking I lander. Part of the lander is seen here in the foreground. The rocks in the middle of the picture are about 1 ft (30 cm) across, and this "stony desert" appearance is typical of about 40 percent of Mars' surface area. Some Martian landforms, however, are more dramatic. Olympus Mons towers 15.5 miles (25 km) high.

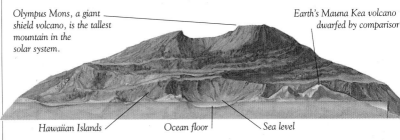

*Olympus Mons, a giant shield volcano, is the tallest mountain in the solar system.*

*Earth's Mauna Kea volcano dwarfed by comparison*

*Hawaiian Islands*  *Ocean floor*  *Sea level*

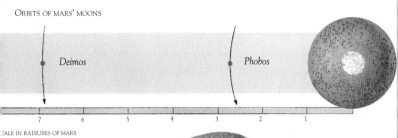

ORBITS OF MARS' MOONS

*Deimos* *Phobos*

SCALE IN RADIUSES OF MARS

7  6  5  4  3  2  1

## SMALL MOONS

Mars has two tiny moons, Phobos and Deimos, neither of them more than 18.5 miles (30 km) in length. Both are irregularly shaped and have every appearance of being asteroids that were captured by Mars' gravity. Phobos orbits Mars at a distance of 5,830 miles (9,380 km) every 7 hours and 40 minutes. Deimos orbits three times farther away, at a distance of 14,581 miles (23,462 km), and takes about 30 hours to circle the planet.

*Smaller and darker than its companion*

DEIMOS

PHOBOS

*The crater Stickney is nearly 6.2 miles (10 km) across*

| MARS: SELECTED EXPLORATION EVENTS | | |
|---|---|---|
| Vehicle | Date | Result |
| Mariner 4 | 7/14/65 | First fly-by images |
| Mars 3 | 12/2/71 | Orbit achieved, lander failed after 20 seconds |
| Mariner 9 | 11/13/71 | Photomapped surface from Martian orbit |
| Viking 1 and | 7/20/76 | Successful soft landings provide images and soil data |
| Viking 2 | 9/3/76 | but no evidence of life |

## MORE FACTS

• Phobos means "fear," and Deimos means "terror" – suitable companions for the planet named after a god of war.

• Viewed from the surface of Mars, Phobos crosses the sky three times each day.

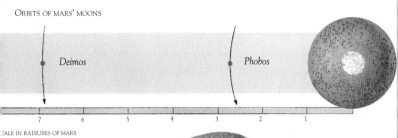MARS

# JUPITER

THE LARGEST of the planets, Jupiter has two and a half times more mass than all the other planets together. Jupiter has a small rock core, but consists mainly of gas in various physical states. The mantle of cold liquefied gas merges into a dense atmosphere. Giant wind systems give Jupiter a banded appearance.

GAS GIANT
Voyager I photographed Jupiter fr a distance of 17.5 million miles (28.4 million km). The moon Io just visible against a background Jupiter's stormy atmosphere.

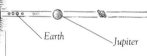

Earth          Jupiter

| JUPITER: PLANETARY DATA | |
| --- | --- |
| Average distance from the Sun | 483.7 million miles (778.3 million km) |
| Orbital period | 11.86 Earth years |
| Orbital velocity | 8.1 miles/sec (13.1 km/s) |
| Rotation period | 9.84 hours |
| Diameter at equator | 88,865 miles (142,984 km) |
| Cloud-top temperature | −238°F (−150°C) |
| Mass (Earth = 1) | 318 |
| Gravity (Earth = 1) | 2.54 |
| Number of moons | 16 |

JUPITER FACTS

• The pressure in Jupiter's interior is so great that hydrogen gas exists naturally in a semisolid metallic form not yet made on Earth.

• Jupiter can be seen with the naked eye as a bright silver "star" in Earth's night sky.

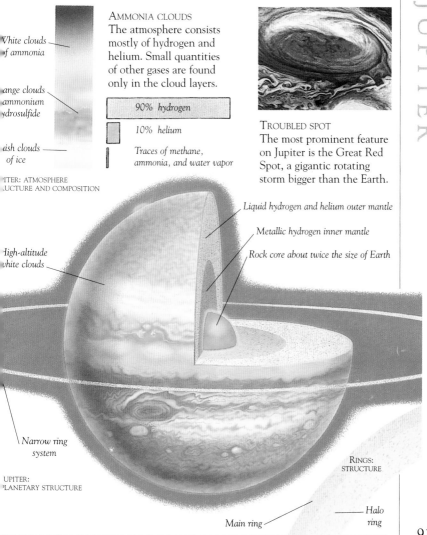

White clouds
of ammonia

Orange clouds
of ammonium
hydrosulfide

Bluish clouds
of ice

JUPITER: ATMOSPHERE
STRUCTURE AND COMPOSITION

High-altitude
white clouds

AMMONIA CLOUDS
The atmosphere consists
mostly of hydrogen and
helium. Small quantities
of other gases are found
only in the cloud layers.

| 90% hydrogen |
| 10% helium |
| Traces of methane, ammonia, and water vapor |

TROUBLED SPOT
The most prominent feature
on Jupiter is the Great Red
Spot, a gigantic rotating
storm bigger than the Earth.

Liquid hydrogen and helium outer mantle

Metallic hydrogen inner mantle

Rock core about twice the size of Earth

Narrow ring
system

JUPITER:
PLANETARY STRUCTURE

RINGS:
STRUCTURE

Halo
ring

Main ring

## FASTEST SPINNER

Despite its enormous size, 11 times the diameter of Earth, Jupiter rotates on its axis faster than any other planet. This high-speed rotation causes the gas giant to bulge around the equator, giving it a slightly oval shape. The rapid rotation also produces the powerful wind systems which divide Jupiter's atmosphere into bands that lie parallel with the equator. The most powerful winds move at speeds of several hundred miles (kilometers) per hour.

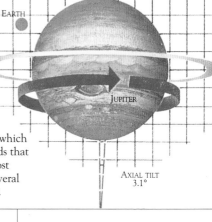

EARTH

JUPITER

AXIAL TILT
3.1°

## THE GALILEAN MOONS:

### EUROPA

Covered by a smooth layer of solid ice, Europa has sufficient internal heat to have seas of liquid water lying beneath its featureless surface.

### CALLISTO

Covered with cracked and dirty ice around a rock core, Callisto is scarred by many craters. The largest is named Valhalla, with a diameter of 1,865 miles (3,000 km).

### GANYMEDE

The largest moon in the solar system, Ganymede is larger than the planets Pluto and Mercury. Believed to consist mainly of ice and slush, Ganymede may have a silicate rock core.

### IO

Debris from many volcanoes gives Io's surface an orange color. The interior is still molten, and Io has the first active volcanoes to be discovered outside the Earth.

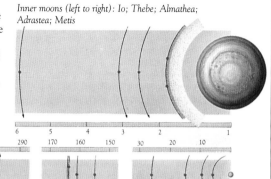

## MOONS OF JUPITER

The four largest moons were discovered by Galileo, hence their collective name. The others have been discovered subsequently, some of them by the Voyager I probe. The four outermost moons orbit in the opposite direction to all the other moons.

*Inner moons (left to right): Io; Thebe; Almathea; Adrastea; Metis*

*Outer moons (left to right): Sinope; Pasiphae; Carme; Ananke; Elara; Lysithea; Himalia; Leda; Callisto; Ganymede; Europa; Io (also shown above)*

SCALE IN RADIUSES OF JUPITER

| JUPITER: SATELLITE DATA | Diameter | | Distance from Jupiter | |
|---|---|---|---|---|
| | miles | km | miles | km |
| Metis | 25 | 40 | 79,528 | 127,960 |
| Adrastea | 12.5 | 20 | 80,162 | 128,980 |
| Almathea | 124 | 200 | 112,679 | 181,300 |
| Thebe | 62 | 100 | 137,912 | 221,900 |
| Io | 2,256 | 3,630 | 262,026 | 421,600 |
| Europa | 1,950 | 3,138 | 416,967 | 670,900 |
| Ganymede | 3,270 | 5,262 | 665,009 | 1,070,000 |
| Callisto | 2,983 | 4,800 | 1,170,292 | 1,883,000 |
| Leda | 10 | 16 | 6,894,966 | 11,094,000 |
| Himalia | 112 | 180 | 7,134,866 | 11,480,000 |
| Lysithea | 25 | 40 | 7,284,027 | 11,720,000 |
| Elara | 50 | 80 | 7,294,592 | 11,737,000 |
| Ananke | 19 | 30 | 13,175,885 | 21,200,000 |
| Carme | 27 | 44 | 14,045,991 | 22,600,000 |
| Pasiphae | 43 | 70 | 14,605,344 | 23,500,000 |
| Sinope | 25 | 40 | 14,729,645 | 23,700,000 |

### MORE FACTS

• The orbital periods of planetary satellites increase according to their distance from the planet. Innermost Metis orbits Jupiter in 0.295 Earth days, while Sinope takes 758 days.

• The Voyager probes obtained 30,000 images of Jupiter and its moons.

• The volcanoes on Io eject material at speeds up to 3,285 ft per sec (1,000 m/s). This is about 20 times faster than material from volcanoes on Earth.

JUPITER

93

# SATURN

FAMED FOR ITS magnificent ring system, Saturn is the second largest of the planets. Like its nearest neighbor Jupiter, Saturn is a gas giant. However, the mass is so spread out that on average the planet is less dense than water. Saturn has more moons than any other planet – at least 18. The largest moon, Titan, has an unusually thick atmosphere.

RINGED WORLD
Saturn is at the limit of easy telescopic viewing from Earth. This photograph was taken at a distance of 11 million miles (17.5 million km) by Voyager 2.

*Earth*          *Saturn*

| SATURN: PLANETARY DATA | |
| --- | --- |
| Average distance from the Sun: | 886.9 million miles 1,427 million km |
| Orbital period | 29.46 Earth years |
| Orbital velocity | 6 miles/sec (9.6 km/s) |
| Rotation period | 10.23 hours |
| Diameter at equator | 74,914 miles (120,536 km) |
| Cloud-top temperature | −292°F (−180°C) |
| Mass (Earth = 1) | 95 |
| Gravity (Earth = 1) | 0.93 |
| Number of moons | 18 |

SATURN FACTS

• Saturn's rings are less than 656 ft (200 m) thick, but over 167,800 miles (270,000 km) in diameter.

• The rings consist of billions of ice-covered rock fragments and dust particles.

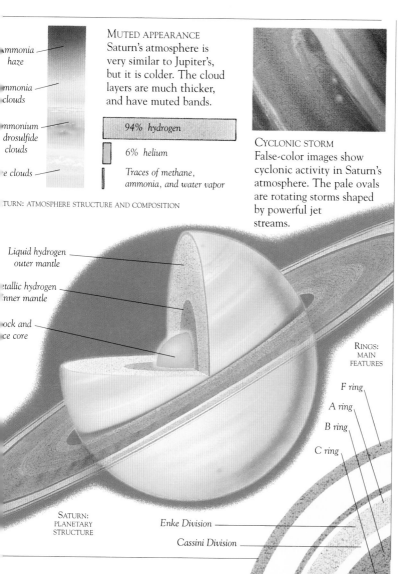

ammonia
haze

ammonia
clouds

ammonium
hydrosulfide
clouds

ice clouds

SATURN: ATMOSPHERE STRUCTURE AND COMPOSITION

MUTED APPEARANCE
Saturn's atmosphere is
very similar to Jupiter's,
but it is colder. The cloud
layers are much thicker,
and have muted bands.

94% hydrogen

6% helium

Traces of methane,
ammonia, and water vapor

CYCLONIC STORM
False-color images show
cyclonic activity in Saturn's
atmosphere. The pale ovals
are rotating storms shaped
by powerful jet
streams.

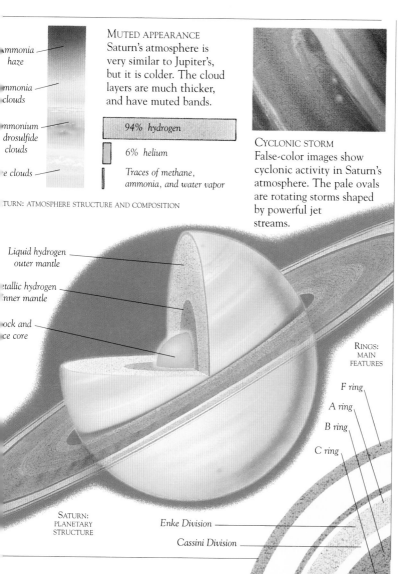

Liquid hydrogen
outer mantle

Metallic hydrogen
inner mantle

Rock and
ice core

RINGS:
MAIN
FEATURES

F ring

A ring

B ring

C ring

SATURN:
PLANETARY
STRUCTURE

Enke Division

Cassini Division

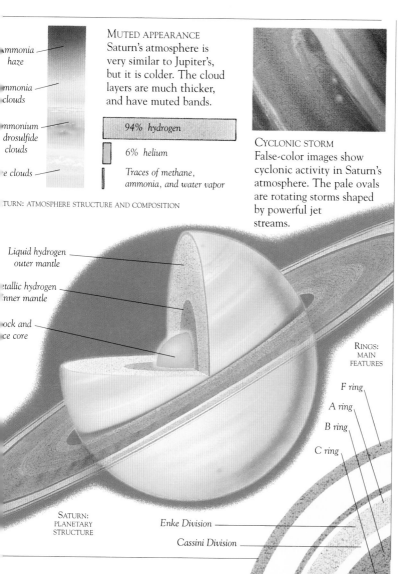

SATURN

95

### TILTED SYSTEM

Saturn rotates very rapidly on an axis that is tilted at 26.7° to the vertical. The orbits of the rings and moons are all aligned with this rotation, and lie in the same plane as the planet's equator, giving the whole system a tilted appearance. Like the other giant gas planets, Saturn bulges noticeably at the equator where the speed of rotation is faster than at the poles. Inside the atmosphere, winds sweep around the equator at 1,120 mph (1,800 km/h).

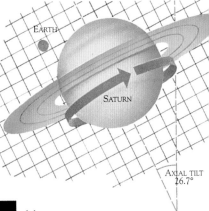

EARTH

SATURN

AXIAL TILT
26.7°

### MANY MOONS

Saturn has 18 moons; one (Titan) is ver large, seven are of average size, and the rest are small and irregularly shaped. Some of the small moons are co-orbital: they share an orbit with another moon. Mimas, the closest of the larger moons, dominated by the huge crater Herschel, perhaps the result of a co-orbital collisic

### BRAIDED RINGS

Some of the inner moons orbi within the rings, creating gap and braids. Pan sweeps the Er Division clear of ring materia while Prometheus and Pandor twist and braid the F ring witl their gravitational effect. The moons are sometimes said to "shepherd" the rings in the same way that dogs keep a flo of sheep together.

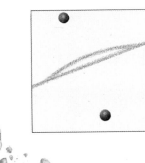

**CROWDED SPACE**
Saturn has both a pair and a triplet of co-orbital moons. In addition, two other moons, Janus and Epithemus, have orbits that are extremely close to each other. Astronomers believe that these two were once a single moon that broke up.

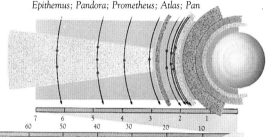

Inner moons (left to right): Helene and Dione (co-orbital); Calypso, Telesto, and Tethys (co-orbital); Enceladus; Mimas; Janus; Epithemus; Pandora; Prometheus; Atlas; Pan

Outer moons (left to right): Phoebe; Iapetus; Hyperion; Titan; Rhea; Helene; and Dione (also shown above)

SCALE IN RADIUSES OF SATURN

### SATURN: SATELLITE FACTS

|  | Diameter | | Distance from Saturn | |
|---|---|---|---|---|
|  | miles | km | miles | km |
| Pan | 12 | 20 | 83,033 | 133,600 |
| Atlas | 21 | 34 | 85,544 | 137,640 |
| Prometheus | 68 | 110 | 86,607 | 139,350 |
| Pandora | 55 | 88 | 88,067 | 141,700 |
| Epimetheus | 75 | 120 | 94,109 | 151,422 |
| Janus | 118 | 190 | 94,140 | 151,472 |
| Mimas | 242 | 390 | 115,301 | 185,520 |
| Enceladus | 311 | 500 | 147,930 | 238,020 |
| Tethys | 653 | 1,050 | 183,132 | 294,660 |
| Telesto | 15 | 25 | 183,132 | 294,660 |
| Calypso | 16 | 26 | 183,132 | 294,660 |
| Dione | 696 | 1,120 | 234,555 | 377,400 |
| Helene | 20 | 33 | 234,555 | 377,400 |
| Rhea | 951 | 1,530 | 327,557 | 527,040 |
| Titan | 3,201 | 5,150 | 759,385 | 1,221,850 |
| Hyperion | 174 | 280 | 920,447 | 1,481,000 |
| Iapetus | 895 | 1,440 | 2,213,362 | 3,561,300 |
| Phoebe | 137 | 220 | 8,049,720 | 12,952,000 |

### MORE FACTS

• The rings of Saturn seem to be neatly graded, with the largest fragments found in the inner rings closest to the planet, while fine dust accumulates in the outer rings.

• Saturn is the only planet that has three moons sharing the same orbit – Tethys, Telesto, and Calypso.

• Mimas was to have been named "Arthur." Although this did not happen, many of its features are named after characters in the legend of King Arthur.

# URANUS

A COLD GAS giant, Uranus is the seventh planet from the Sun. Little surface detail can be seen, and even close-up pictures show only a few clouds of frozen methane gas. Despite its featureless appearance, Uranus has one interesting peculiarity. The planet, and its rings and moons, are all tilted by more than 90°, traveling around the Sun on their side.

BLANK FACE
Faintly visible from Earth as a dim "star" in the night sky, Uranus was not identified as a planet until 1781. The ring system was not discovered until 1977 – almost 200 years later.

*Earth*

*Uranus*

| URANUS: PLANETARY DATA | |
| --- | --- |
| Average distance from the Sun | 1,784 million miles (2,871 million km) |
| Orbital period | 84 Earth years |
| Orbital velocity | 4.2 miles/sec (6.8 km/s) |
| Rotation period | 17.9 hours |
| Diameter at equator | 31,770 miles (51,118 km) |
| Cloud-top temperature | −346°F (−210°C) |
| Mass (Earth = 1) | 14.5 |
| Gravity (Earth = 1) | 0.79 |
| Number of moons | 15 |

URANUS FACTS

• Uranus is named after Urania, the Greek muse (patron goddess) of astronomy.

• Light from the Sun, which takes about eight minutes to reach Earth, takes more than 2 hours 30 minutes to travel as far as Uranus.

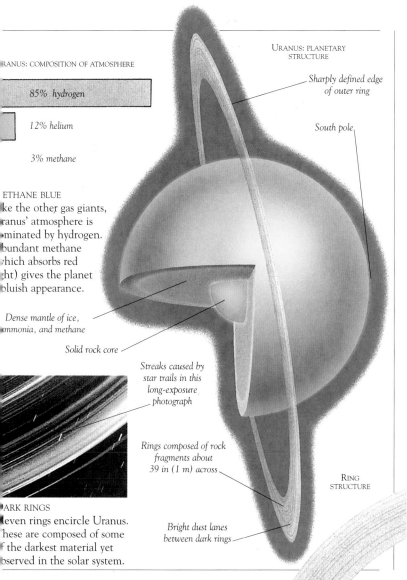

RANUS: COMPOSITION OF ATMOSPHERE

85% hydrogen

12% helium

3% methane

ETHANE BLUE
ke the other gas giants,
ranus' atmosphere is
minated by hydrogen.
bundant methane
which absorbs red
ght) gives the planet
bluish appearance.

*Dense mantle of ice,
ammonia, and methane*

*Solid rock core*

URANUS: PLANETARY
STRUCTURE

*Sharply defined edge
of outer ring*

*South pole*

*Streaks caused by
star trails in this
long-exposure
photograph*

*Rings composed of rock
fragments about
39 in (1 m) across*

RING
STRUCTURE

*Bright dust lanes
between dark rings*

ARK RINGS
leven rings encircle Uranus.
hese are composed of some
f the darkest material yet
bserved in the solar system.

## SIDEWAYS ORBIT

Uranus' axis of rotation is tilted at 98° to the vertical – the equator runs through the "top" and "bottom" of the planet. This extreme tilt also extends to the rings and moons. Uranus' sideways stance may have been the result of a collision with another celestial body at some time in the distant past.

EARTH

AXIAL TILT 98°

URANUS

## LENGTHY SEASONS

Uranus' peculiar tilt creates extremely long seasons. As the planet travels around the Sun, each pole receives 42 Earth years of sunlight, followed by the same period of total darkness. However, the temperature does not vary with the seasons because Uranus is so far away from the Sun.

## STRANGE MAGNETISM

Uranus generates a magnetic field which is tilted, but not the same way as the planet. The magnetic field is tilted at 60° to the axis of rotation, which means that the magnetosphere has a fairly normal shape. To make the situation even more extraordinary, Uranus' magnetic field is offset from the planet's center.

RINGS AND MOONS
Only the innermost
moon, Cordelia,
orbits within the ring
system. Miranda is
perhaps the most
unusual moon in the
solar system – it
shows every sign of
once having been
blasted apart and
then reassembled.

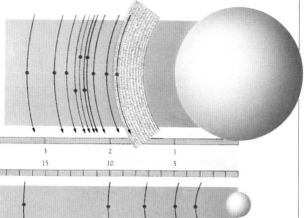

*Inner moons (left to right): Puck; Belinda; Rosalind; Portia; Juliet; Desdemona; Cressida; Bianca; Ophelia; Cordelia*

25   20   15   10   5
4   3   2   1

*Outer moons (left to right): Oberon; Titania; Umbriel; Ariel; Miranda; Puck (also shown above)*

## URANUS: SATELLITE DATA

|  | Diameter | | Distance from Uranus | |
|---|---|---|---|---|
|  | miles | km | miles | km |
| Cordelia | 19 | 30 | 30,920 | 49,750 |
| Ophelia | 19 | 30 | 33,412 | 53,760 |
| Bianca | 25 | 40 | 36,768 | 59,160 |
| Cressida | 43 | 70 | 38,390 | 61,770 |
| Desdemona | 37 | 60 | 38,943 | 62,660 |
| Juliet | 50 | 80 | 40,000 | 64,360 |
| Portia | 68 | 110 | 41,081 | 66,100 |
| Rosalind | 37 | 60 | 43,462 | 69,930 |
| Belinda | 43 | 70 | 46,774 | 75,260 |
| Puck | 93 | 150 | 53,456 | 86,010 |
| Miranda | 292 | 470 | 80,659 | 129,780 |
| Ariel | 721 | 1,160 | 118,856 | 191,240 |
| Umbriel | 727 | 1,170 | 165,301 | 265,970 |
| Titania | 982 | 1,580 | 270,876 | 435,840 |
| Oberon | 945 | 1,520 | 362,088 | 582,600 |

## MORE FACTS

• Before Voyager 2, Uranus was believed to have five moons. The accepted total is now 15, and there may be more waiting to be discovered.

• The Uranian moons are all named after characters in plays by William Shakespeare.

• In contrast to Saturn, the outermost Uranian ring has no fragments less than about 8 in (20 cm) across.

# NEPTUNE

THE OUTERMOST of the gas giants, Neptune is a near twin to Uranus. Too faint to be seen easily from Earth, its position was calculated mathematically. Neptune was first observed in 1846 exactly where it was predicted to be. Methane in the atmosphere gives Neptune a deep blue coloration. The rings and six of the moons were discovered by the Voyager 2 probe.

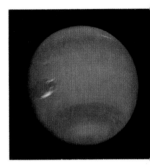

DARK STORMS
Photographed by the second Voyager probe, the atmosphere of Neptune shows several clear features including the Great Dark Spot, which is a huge cyclonic storm.

_Earth_

_Neptune_

NEPTUNE: PLANETARY DATA

| | |
|---|---|
| Average distance from the Sun | 2,795 million miles (4,497 million km) |
| Orbital period | 164.8 Earth years |
| Orbital velocity | 3.4 miles/sec (5.4 km/s) |
| Rotation period | 19.2 hours |
| Diameter at equator | 30,782 miles (49,528 km) |
| Cloud-top temperature | −364°F (−220°C) |
| Mass (Earth = 1) | 17 |
| Gravity (Earth = 1) | 1.2 |
| Number of moons | 8 |

NEPTUNE FACTS

• Neptune is named after the Roman god of the sea.
• Neptune radiates 2.6 times more heat than it receives from the Sun – a sign of an internal source of heat.

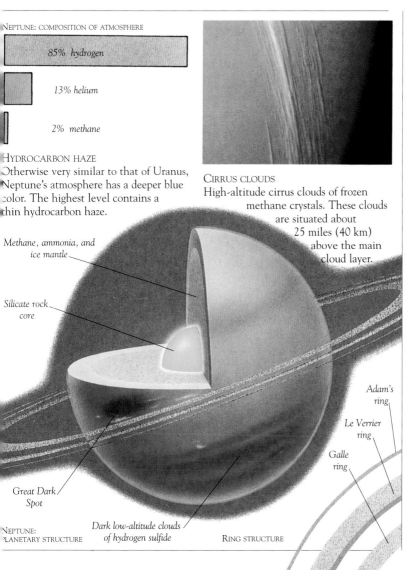

NEPTUNE: COMPOSITION OF ATMOSPHERE

85% hydrogen

13% helium

2% methane

HYDROCARBON HAZE
Otherwise very similar to that of Uranus,
Neptune's atmosphere has a deeper blue
color. The highest level contains a
thin hydrocarbon haze.

CIRRUS CLOUDS
High-altitude cirrus clouds of frozen
methane crystals. These clouds
are situated about
25 miles (40 km)
above the main
cloud layer.

Methane, ammonia, and
ice mantle

Silicate rock
core

Adam's
ring

Le Verrier
ring

Galle
ring

Great Dark
Spot

NEPTUNE:
PLANETARY STRUCTURE

Dark low-altitude clouds
of hydrogen sulfide

RING STRUCTURE

### LACK OF SEASONS

Neptune rotates on its axis at approximately the same angle of tilt as Earth. However, Neptune is far too distant from the Sun for the tilt to result in a similar cycle of seasons. Conditions in the atmosphere are dominated by winds blowing at up to 1,250 mph (2,000 km/s) which carry the dark storms around the planet in a backward direction.

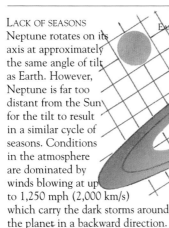

EARTH

NEPTUNE

AXIAL TILT
29.6°

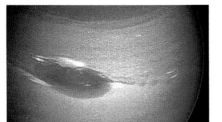

### GREAT DARK SPOT

The largest storm on Neptune, the Great Dark Spot is about the same size as Earth. The storm rotates in an counterclockwise direction. This photograph has been processed to give a red color to high-altitude features.

### TRITON

The largest of Neptune's moons, Triton is the coldest place in the solar system at –391°F (–235°C). It has a thin atmosphere, mainly of nitrogen, and a large south polar ice cap composed of methane ice. Photographs show the ice to have a pink tinge, which is believed to be due to the presence of organic chemicals formed by the action of sunlight.

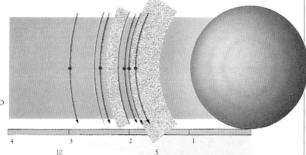

*Inner moons (left to right): Larissa; Galatea; Despina; Thalassa; Naiad*

CIRCLING NEPTUNE
The four innermost
moons orbit within
the ring system.
Triton is the only
large moon in the
solar system that
orbits in a backward
direction compared to
the planet's rotation.

SCALE IN RADIUSES OF NEPTUNE

*Outer moons (left to right): Nereid; Triton; Proteus; Larissa; and inner moons (also shown above)*

DISTANT EXPLORER

Voyager 2 is the only probe that has so far visited
Uranus and Neptune. The journey to Neptune took 12
years, and information from Voyager 2 (transmitted at
the speed of light) took more than four hours to reach
Earth. Among Voyager 2's many discoveries were six of
Neptune's eight moons and ice volcanoes on Triton.

VOYAGER 2

NEPTUNE: SATELLITE DATA

|  | Diameter | | Distance from Neptune | |
|---|---|---|---|---|
|  | miles | km | miles | km |
| Naiad | 31 | 50 | 29,832 | 48,000 |
| Thalassa | 50 | 80 | 31,075 | 50,000 |
| Despina | 112 | 180 | 32,629 | 52,500 |
| Galatea | 93 | 150 | 38,533 | 62,000 |
| Larissa | 118 | 190 | 45,743 | 73,600 |
| Proteus | 249 | 400 | 73,088 | 117,600 |
| Triton | 1,678 | 2,700 | 220,510 | 354,800 |
| Nereid | 211 | 340 | 3,426,600 | 5,513,400 |

FACT

• The outermost moon,
Nereid, has the most
eccentric orbit of any
known satellite. During
a single orbit, Nereid's
distance from Neptune
varies between 800,000
miles (1,300,000 km)
and 6,000,000 miles
(9,700,000 km).

# PLUTO

THE MOST DISTANT of all the planets, Pluto, is also the least understood. Pluto's orbit around the Sun is uniquely tilted at 17°, and is highly unusual in other ways. For about ten percent of its long orbital path, Pluto is closer to the Sun than Neptune. Pluto has a single large moon, Charon, and together they form a two-object system.

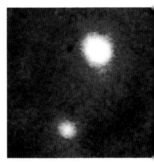

BLURRED IMAGE
The clearest image of Pluto and Charon has been obtained by the Hubble Space Telescope orbiting Earth. Ground-based photographs show a single blur.

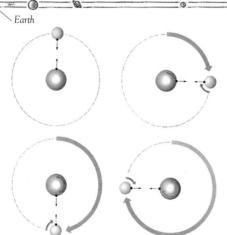

Earth

Pluto

CLOSELY LINKED SYSTEM
Pluto and Charon exhibit a powerful effect on each other. Charon's orbit around Pluto has become synchronized with Pluto's own rotation, so that both have the same period – 6. Earth days. As a result, the same face of Charon is always turned to the same face of Pluto. From one side of Pluto, Charon is always visible in the sky. From the other side of the planet, the moon cannot be seen at all.

## PLUTO: PLANETARY DATA

| | |
|---|---|
| Average distance from the Sun | 3.675 billion miles (5.955 billion km) |
| Orbital period | 248.5 Earth years |
| Orbital velocity | 2.9 miles/sec (4.7 kms) |
| Rotation period | 6.38 Earth days |
| Diameter at equator | 1,429 miles (2,300 km) |
| Surface temperature | −382°F (−230°C) |
| Mass (Earth = 1) | 0.002 |
| Gravity (Earth = 1) | 0.04            Moons: 1 |

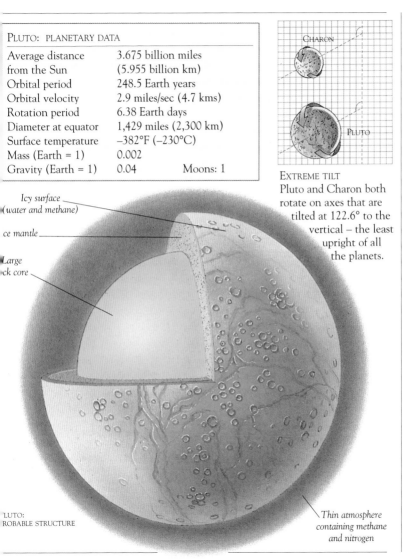

CHARON

PLUTO

**EXTREME TILT**
Pluto and Charon both rotate on axes that are tilted at 122.6° to the vertical – the least upright of all the planets.

*Icy surface (water and methane)*

*Ice mantle*

*Large rock core*

PLUTO: PROBABLE STRUCTURE

*Thin atmosphere containing methane and nitrogen*

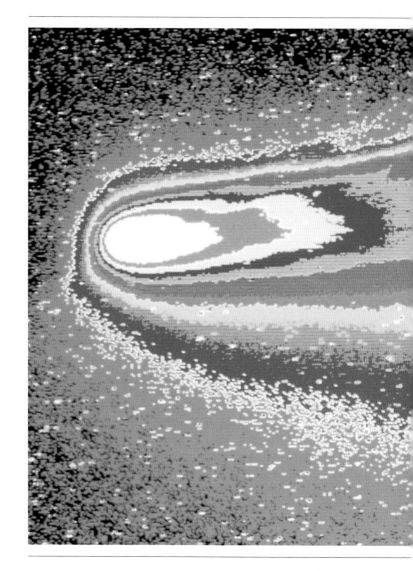

# SMALL OBJECTS

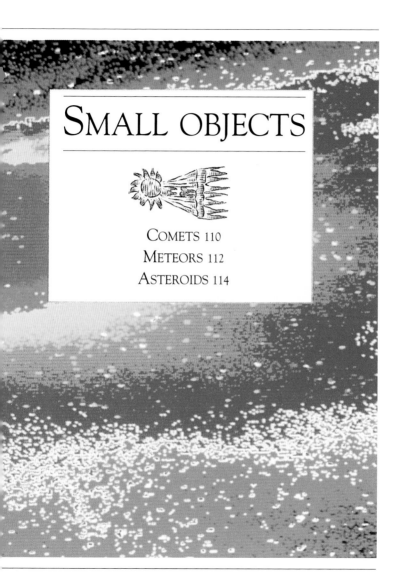

# COMETS

A COMET IS a "dirty snowball" composed of snow and dust. Billions of comets orbit the Sun at a distance of about one light year. A few comets have orbits that take them closer to the Sun. As they near the Sun and are heated, the snow turns to gas and forms a long bright tail.

COMET HALLEY
Most comets that approach the Sun are seen only once, but a few return periodically. Comet Halley returns every 76 years.

ORBITING THE SUN
A periodic comet has a regular orbit that brings it close to the Sun. For most of its orbit, the comet has no tail. The tail only develops as the comet nears the Sun and its surface is heated. The tail gets longer and longer, and then disappears as the comet moves away from the Sun.

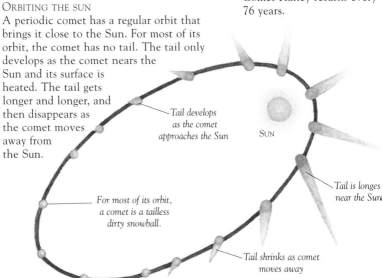

*Tail develops as the comet approaches the Sun*

SUN

*Tail is longest near the Sun*

*For most of its orbit, a comet is a tailless dirty snowball.*

*Tail shrinks as comet moves away*

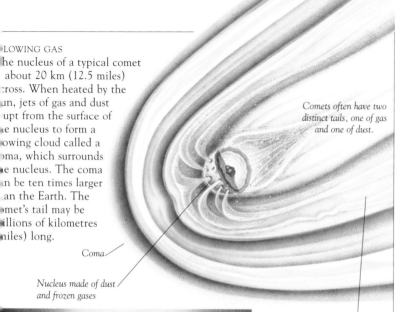

### GLOWING GAS

The nucleus of a typical comet is about 20 km (12.5 miles) across. When heated by the Sun, jets of gas and dust erupt from the surface of the nucleus to form a glowing cloud called a coma, which surrounds the nucleus. The coma can be ten times larger than the Earth. The comet's tail may be millions of kilometres (miles) long.

*Comets often have two distinct tails, one of gas and one of dust.*

*Coma*

*Nucleus made of dust and frozen gases*

*Dust reflects sunlight*

### HEART OF A COMET

This photograph of the nucleus of Comet Halley was taken by the Giotto probe from a distance of about 1,700 km (1,050 miles). Bright gas jets can be seen on the sunlit (upper) surface. Instruments aboard Giotto showed that the main constituent of the nucleus was water-ice.

### COMET FACT

• The planet Jupiter is so massive that its gravity can affect the orbit of comets. In 1993, Comet Shoemaker-Levy passed close to Jupiter and was broken into several fragments by gravitational forces. During July 1994, these fragments crashed into Jupiter, causing a series of huge explosions in Jupiter's atmosphere.

# METEORS

EVERY DAY, thousands of dust particles and rock fragments from space enter the Earth's atmosphere. Most burn up due to friction with the air. The streaks of light they produce are called meteors. Very rarely a larger fragment survives the atmosphere and hits Earth's surface. These "space-rocks" are called meteorites.

METEOR SHOWER
This is a a false-color photograph of a Leonid meteor shower (yellow streaks), which is associated with Comet Tempel Tuttle.

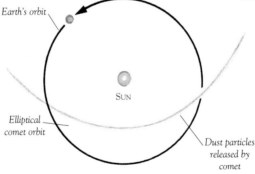

Earth's orbit

SUN

Elliptical comet orbit

Dust particles released by comet

CROSSING ORBITS
Most meteors are caused by dust and debris shed by comets as they pass close to the Sun. The debris stays in the path of the comet's orbit; and when the Earth's orbit crosses that of the comet, we experience a meteor shower. Some showers are regular annual events.

METEOR FACTS

• Each year about 28,000 tons (tonnes) of extra-terrestrial material enters our atmosphere.

• Most meteors are vaporized at altitudes above 50 miles (80 km).

• Meteor showers are named after the constellation in which the radiant appears, e.g. the Perseids.

• The heaviest showers have meteors falling at 60,000 per hour.

STONY METEORITE

*Fragments of nickel-iron embedded in a matrix of rock*

*Heat-blackened surface*

STONY-IRON METEORITE

### STONES AND IRONS FROM SPACE

There are two main types of meteorite – those composed mainly of rock (called "stones") and those made mostly of metal (called "irons"). Rocky meteorites are far more common than "irons," but the rarest meteorites on Earth (less than one in every hundred found) are "stony-irons" that contain both metal and rock.

### IMPACT CRATER

Meteorite Crater in Arizona measures 0.8 miles (1.3 km) across. It was formed about 25,000 years ago when a meteorite about 150 ft (45 m) in diameter struck the surface at a speed of around 8 miles/sec (11 km/s). Meteorite hunters have found several "iron" fragments in the crater.

### METEORITE FACTS

• More than 90% of identified meteorites that strike the Earth are "stones."

• The world's largest known meteorite still lies where it fell at Hoba West in southern Africa. Its weight is estimated at over 60 tons (tonnes).

• Last century, Czar Alexander of Russia had a sword made from an "iron" meteorite.

113

# ASTEROIDS

MILLIONS OF CHUNKS of rock orbit the Sun. These are the asteroids, sometimes called the minor planets. Asteroids range in size from a few feet (meters) across, to those that are hundreds of miles (kilometers) in diameter. Most of the asteroids are found in a wide belt between the orbits of Mars and Jupiter.

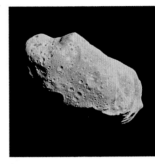

SPACE ROCK
Ida is a typical asteroid – small and irregular in shape with a maximum length of 32 miles (52 km). Its surface is heavily cratered and covered by a thin layer of dust.

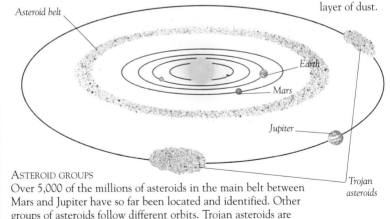

Asteroid belt

Earth

Mars

Jupiter

Trojan asteroids

ASTEROID GROUPS
Over 5,000 of the millions of asteroids in the main belt between Mars and Jupiter have so far been located and identified. Other groups of asteroids follow different orbits. Trojan asteroids are co-orbital with Jupiter, held in place by the giant planet's powerful gravity.

*Craters due to meteorite impacts*

*Most asteroids are irregular in shape.*

*coloration*
*use surface is*
*ered in rust*

### ASTEROID ORIGINS

The larger asteroids are spherical and were formed in the same way as the planets. The smaller irregular asteroids are either remnants of the original material that formed the solar system, or the result of collisions between two or more large asteroids.

### FAILED PLANET

The asteroid belt was probably formed at the same time as the rest of the solar system. Rock fragments and dust particles in this part of the system were prevented from clumping together to form a planet by Jupiter's gravity. But if all the asteroids were put together, their mass would be only a tiny fraction of the Earth's.

### ASTEROID FACTS

The first asteroid to e discovered was Ceres which has a diameter of 80 miles (933 km).

Asteroids which have n average distance om the Sun less than arth's are known as ten asteroids.

Earth has been struck y several asteroids in he past, and it is only a atter of time before nother asteroid strikes ur planet.

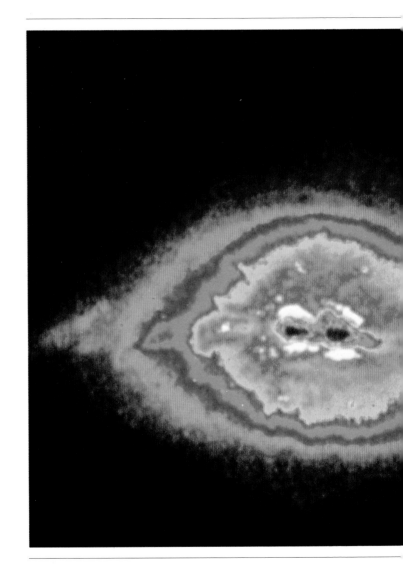

# STUDYING SPACE

# INFORMATION FROM SPACE

GATHERING AND STUDYING starlight is just one way that we learn about the universe. Visible light is only a small part of the electromagnetic spectrum, which covers all forms of radiation. By studying different types of radiation, we learn more about both the visible and the invisible parts of the universe.

Ozone layer

Gamma rays and X-rays

UV rays

Most infrared stopped here

Visible light and short-wave radio reach surface

ATMOSPHERIC SHIELD
The atmosphere shields Earth against radiation from space. Gamma rays, X-rays, and most ultraviolet (UV) rays are stopped. Only visible light, some infrared and UV radiation, and some radio signals reach the surface.

INFORMATION SPECTRUM
Electromagnetic radiation travels through space as waves of varying length (the distance between wave crests). Gamma rays have the shortest wavelength, then X-rays, and so on through the spectrum to the longest radio waves. Visible light, which is all that we can see naturally, occupies a very narrow portion (less than 0.00001 percent) of the spectrum.

$10^{-13}$ m
0.0000000000001 meters

X-RAYS

GAMMA RAYS

118

## CRAB NEBULA IN DIFFERENT LIGHTS

The Crab Nebula is the remnant of a supernova explosion seen in 1054. In UV light (right) the nebula has an eerie glow produced by highly energetic particles from the explosion interacting with the surrounding space environment.

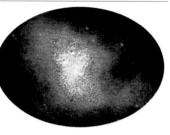

### VISIBLE LIGHT

This visible light image of the nebula has been computer-processed to show the presence of hydrogen (red) and sulfur (blue) in the filaments of gas still streaming out from the explosion.

### X-RAY

X-rays emitted by the Crab Nebula produce a picture (right) that shows a bright object at the center of the nebula – the pulsar that is the remains of the presupernova star.

$10^{-7}$ m
0.0000001 meters

$10^5$ m
100,000 meters

VISIBLE LIGHT

MICROWAVES

AVIOLET
GHT

INFRARED LIGHT

RADIO WAVES

# OPTICAL TELESCOPES

THE OPTICAL TELESCOPE is one of the main tools of astronomy. But little time is spent looking through a telescope eyepiece – modern instruments collect and store visual information electronically. The optical telescope remains an important tool because it gathers basic information.

PALOMAR DOME
The protective dome of the Hale Telescope at the Mount Palomar Observatory, California, shields the telescope from the effects of weather.

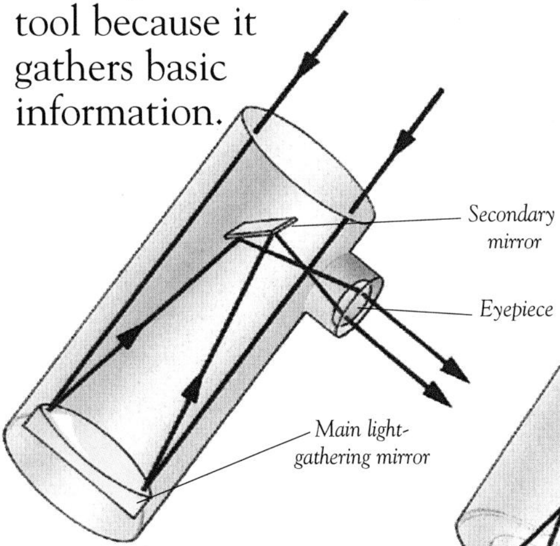

Secondary mirror

Eyepiece

Main light-gathering lens

Eyepiece lens

Main light-gathering mirror

REFLECTOR TELESCOPES
Telescopes use lenses and mirrors to gather light and produce an image. Reflector telescopes, which make use of curved mirrors, are the most useful type for astronomy.

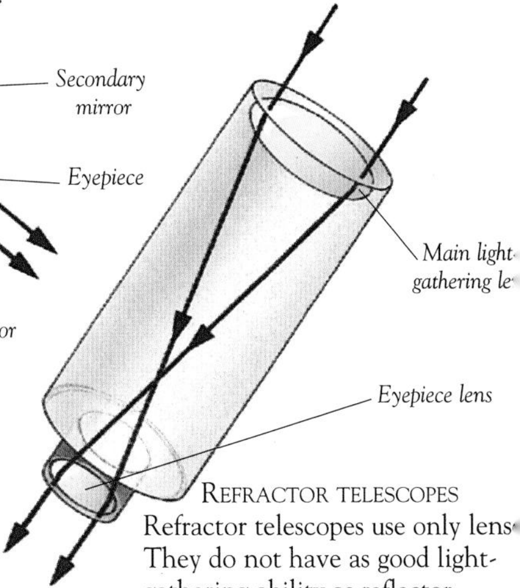

REFRACTOR TELESCOPES
Refractor telescopes use only lenses. They do not have as good light-gathering ability as reflector telescopes, but they remain very popular with amateur astronomers.

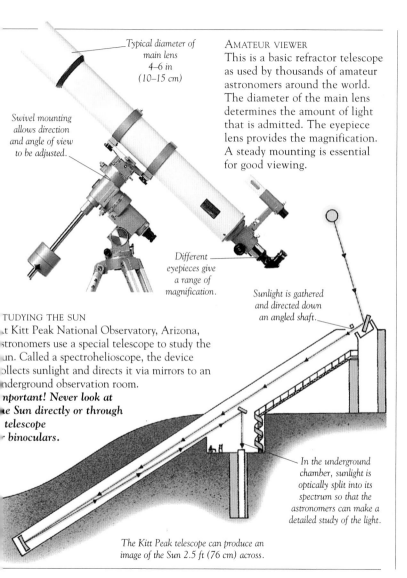

Typical diameter of
main lens
4–6 in
(10–15 cm)

Swivel mounting
allows direction
and angle of view
to be adjusted.

AMATEUR VIEWER
This is a basic refractor telescope
as used by thousands of amateur
astronomers around the world.
The diameter of the main lens
determines the amount of light
that is admitted. The eyepiece
lens provides the magnification.
A steady mounting is essential
for good viewing.

Different
eyepieces give
a range of
magnification.

Sunlight is gathered
and directed down
an angled shaft.

STUDYING THE SUN
At Kitt Peak National Observatory, Arizona,
astronomers use a special telescope to study the
Sun. Called a spectrohelioscope, the device
collects sunlight and directs it via mirrors to an
underground observation room.
**Important! Never look at
the Sun directly or through
a telescope
or binoculars.**

In the underground
chamber, sunlight is
optically split into its
spectrum so that the
astronomers can make a
detailed study of the light.

The Kitt Peak telescope can produce an
image of the Sun 2.5 ft (76 cm) across.

# RADIO ASTRONOMY

WE HAVE BEEN LISTENING in to the radio energy of the universe for about 50 years. Radio astronomy can obtain additional information about familiar objects, as well as seek out new ones. Two major discoveries – quasars and pulsars – were made by radio astronomers.

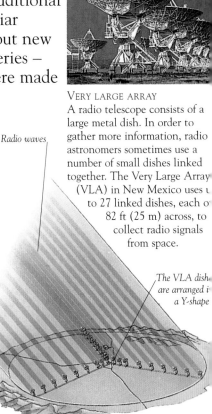

VERY LARGE ARRAY
A radio telescope consists of a large metal dish. In order to gather more information, radio astronomers sometimes use a number of small dishes linked together. The Very Large Array (VLA) in New Mexico uses up to 27 linked dishes, each of 82 ft (25 m) across, to collect radio signals from space.

*Radio waves*

*The VLA dishes are arranged in a Y-shape*

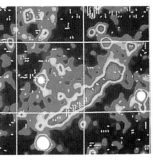

RADIO VISION
Radio telescopes, like ordinary radio sets, can be tuned to a particular wavelength, and the intensity of the radio energy can be measured. Computers are then used to produce "radio-maps" of the sky, such as this image of the bar-shaped radio source known as 1952+28.

### Largest dish

The world's largest radio telescope, the 1,000 ft (305 m) Arecibo dish, is built into a natural hollow in the hills of Puerto Rico. The dish is "steered" using the Earth's own rotation. Arecibo has also been used to send a radio message out into space.

*Simple processing of the Arecibo message produces this visual image which contains a representation of a human being.*

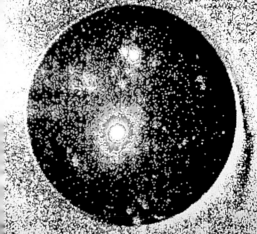

### Radio galaxies

Many galaxies that are quite faint visually are very "bright" at radio wavelengths. These are often called radio galaxies, or active galaxies. This optical image of radio galaxy 3C 33 has been color-coded according to the intensity of light in the visible part of the spectrum – ranging from white (most intense) to blue (the least).

# IMAGES OF SPACE

MUCH OF THE information that astronomers obtain through their instruments is presented as visual images. Conventional and electronic cameras are used to record these images. The information is usually stored on computers which can process images to improve the picture and bring out details.

PIXELATED VIEW
Electronic cameras make images with a grid of tiny picture-elements (pixels). This view of a dim and distant star cluster was obtained with a ground-based telescope. The individual pixels are clearly visible, although it takes a trained eye to identify the image as a star cluster.

MARTIAN CHEMICAL PHOTOMAP
This image of the surface of Mars, with the Martian equator running across the middle of the picture, was produced by cameras aboard the Viking orbiter space probes. The image has been color-coded by computer according to the chemical composition of the surface. Craters and other surface features are also visible.

*Frost is shown in turquoise*

*Red identifies high concentrations of iron oxide*

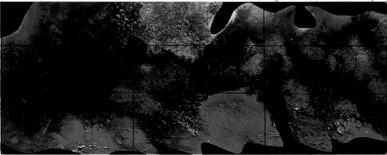

FALSE COLOR GIVES A TRUER VIEW
Astronomers have several techniques for
analysing the information contained in
images. One of the most important is
adding false color to the image. Saturn
has a fairly muted appearance in
ordinary photographs. This image has
been color-coded to emphasize
the banding of the planet's
upper atmosphere.

COLORING THE CORONA
This image of the normally
invisible solar corona (the Sun's
outer atmosphere) was produced
from data obtained by the Solar
Maximum Mission satellite. The
image has been computer-
processed and enhanced with
false colors, in order to identify
zones of differing gas density
within the solar corona.

SEPARATE THEN COMBINE
Images of space are often obtained through a series
of colored filters. The object is photographed
through each filter in turn, and the resulting images
are then combined to give a much fuller picture
than with any single ordinary photograph. This
series was taken with the Hubble Space Telescope,
and shows Pluto and its moon Charon.

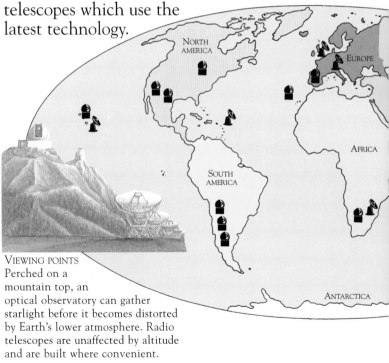

# OBSERVATORIES

OPTICAL TELESCOPES are usually installed in mountain-top observatories, where they suffer the least interference from Earth's atmosphere. Radio telescopes can be situated almost anywhere, and are usually located near universities. Observatories are often shared between countries because of the high cost of telescopes which use the latest technology.

NORTH
AMERICA

EUROPE

SOUTH
AMERICA

AFRICA

ANTARCTICA

VIEWING POINTS
Perched on a mountain top, an optical observatory can gather starlight before it becomes distorted by Earth's lower atmosphere. Radio telescopes are unaffected by altitude and are built where convenient.

## HIGH AND DRY

The domes of the Cerro Tololo Inter-American Observatory are sited in the Andes foothills of Chile. A dry climate with cloud-free nights and a steady atmosphere makes this an ideal location for clear viewing.

### OBSERVATORY FACTS

• The oldest existing observatory was built in South Korea in AD 632.

• There is a flying telescope – the Kuiper Airborne Observatory, a modified C-141 cargo aircraft fitted with a 36 in (91 cm) telescope.

• The 36 elements of the Keck reflector make a mirror 396 in (1,000 cm) across.

• The world's highest observatory is located near Boulder, Colorado, 14,110 ft (4,297 m) above sea level.

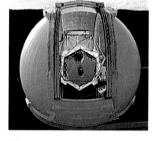

### HIGH-TECH TELESCOPE

The Keck Telescope situated on Mauna Kea, Hawaii, is the world's largest optical telescope. The main mirror is made up of 36 computer-controlled hexagonal segments.

AUSTRALASIA

MAP KEY

OPTICAL TELESCOPE

RADIO TELESCOPE

# TELESCOPES IN SPACE

BY PLACING THEIR TELESCOPES in orbit above Earth's atmosphere, astronomers get a much better view. They can see farther and can collect information from wavelengths that are absorbed by the atmosphere. Information and images gathered in orbit are transmitted back to Earth for study and analysis.

ORBITING TELESCOPE
The US space station Skylab carried a total of eigh telescopes on the X-shaped Apollo Telescope Mounting

*Large solar panels power the equipment aboard the HST.*

*Antenna transmits information to Earth via a communications satellite*

*Protective hinged cover*

NASA

esa

HUBBLE
The Hubble Space Telescope (HST) uses a larg mirror to gather light. The light is then directed by a secondary mirror into one of the scientific instrument packages or high-resolution cameras aboard this orbiting space telescop

*Cameras and instruments located inside*

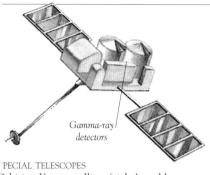

Gamma-ray detectors

Orbiting X-ray satellites (right) enable
scientists to pinpoint areas of intense activity
in distant galaxies. Special telescopes, known
as grazing incidence telescopes, are used
because X-rays pass straight through
conventional lenses and mirrors.

### DIRECTION FINDER
Orbiting gamma-ray telescopes
(left) have been in use since the
mid-1970s. Although gamma rays
cannot be focused to produce an
image, they can be used to plot
the direction and intensity of
gamma-ray sources.

Solar panel

### DUAL USE
The HST (right) operates at the wavelength
of visible light, and also at the slightly shorter
ultraviolet (UV) wavelength. This
feature makes the HST doubly useful
to astronomers as data and images
obtained at two different
wavelengths can be compared.

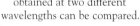

Gold-plated sunshield
cuts out unwanted
infrared radiation

Access panel
for guidance
package

### CLEARER VIEW
From orbit, infrared telescopes (left)
gather infrared light before it can be
absorbed by Earth's lower atmosphere.
Infrared satellites are also used to study
the Earth's surface.

# ROCKETS

SATELLITES, SPACE PROBES, and astronauts are lifted into space by rockets. There are two main types. The conventional tall, thin rocket is made from several stages stacked on top of each other. The newer Space Shuttle design lifts off with the aid of massive booster rockets. But when it returns from space, the Shuttle lands like an aircraft.

LIFTOFF
A Saturn V rocket stands poised on the launch-pad. Its engines burn fuel at a rate of thousands of gallons (liters) per second

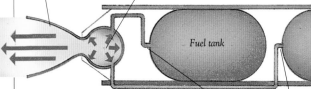

*Nozzle shapes the stream of hot exhaust gases*

*Liquid fuel and oxygen are combined in the combustion chamber.*

Fuel tank

Oxygen tank

*Fuel and oxygen stored in reinforced pressurised tanks*

*Pumps control the flow of fuel and oxygen to the combustion chamber.*

ROCKET POWER
A rocket is propelled upward by hot exhaust gases streaming from nozzles at the tail. These gases are the result of burning a mixture of liquid oxygen and fuel (such as liquid hydrogen) inside a combustion chamber. Carrying its own oxygen supply enables a rocket engine to function in the airless vacuum of space.

## ESCAPE VELOCITY

A rocket, or any other object, is held on the Earth's surface by the force of gravity. To escape the effects of Earth's gravity and enter space, a rocket needs to achieve a speed of 24,840 mph (40,000 km/h) – this is the "escape velocity" of planet Earth. On the Moon, where the force of gravity is only one sixth as powerful as on Earth, the escape velocity is lower – only about 5,300 mph (8,500 km/h).

*Payload – satellite or space probe*

*Third-stage rocket engines*

ARIANE: A TYPICAL THREE-STAGE LAUNCH VEHICLE

*Second-stage rocket engines*

*First-stage rocket engines*

*External booster rockets assist first stage engines at liftoff*

EUSABLE SPACE CRAFT

streaming exhaust trail marks the beginning
another Space Shuttle mission. Unlike
onventional rockets, which can be used only
ce, the Shuttle is reusable. The massive fuel
nk and booster rockets are jettisoned shortly
ter launch and recovered. The Shuttle's own
ngines carry it on into orbit, and small thruster
ckets are used to maneuver it into position.

R O C K E T S

131

# FLY-BYS

LIFTED INTO SPACE by rockets, space probes are computer-controlled robots packed with scientific instruments. Probes are sent to fly by a planet, or even orbit around it, sending data and images back to Earth. After they have completed their planned missions, some probes continue on into space.

VOLCANIC DISCOVERY
The probe Voyager I obtained this image of Io which shows the first active volcano seen outside Earth.

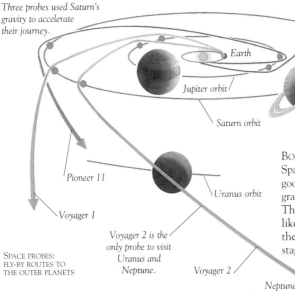

*Three probes used Saturn's gravity to accelerate their journey.*

Earth

Jupiter orbit

Saturn orbit

Pioneer 1‹ left the solar syste‹ after passing Jupite‹

Pioneer 11

Uranus orbit

Voyager 1

*Voyager 2 is the only probe to visit Uranus and Neptune.*

Voyager 2

Neptune

SPACE PROBES:
FLY-BY ROUTES TO
THE OUTER PLANETS

BOOSTED BY GRAVITY
Space probes can make good use of a planet's gravity as they fly by. The pull of gravity act like a sling, acceleratin the probe for the next stage of its journey.

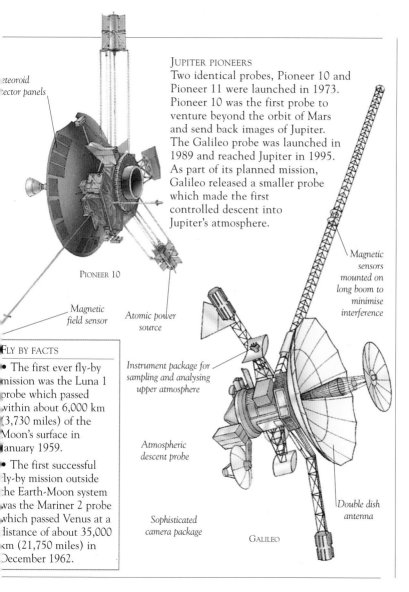

## JUPITER PIONEERS

Two identical probes, Pioneer 10 and Pioneer 11 were launched in 1973. Pioneer 10 was the first probe to venture beyond the orbit of Mars and send back images of Jupiter. The Galileo probe was launched in 1989 and reached Jupiter in 1995. As part of its planned mission, Galileo released a smaller probe which made the first controlled descent into Jupiter's atmosphere.

*Meteoroid detector panels*

PIONEER 10

*Magnetic field sensor*

*Atomic power source*

*Magnetic sensors mounted on long boom to minimise interference*

*Instrument package for sampling and analysing upper atmosphere*

*Atmospheric descent probe*

*Sophisticated camera package*

GALILEO

*Double dish antenna*

### FLY BY FACTS

• The first ever fly-by mission was the Luna 1 probe which passed within about 6,000 km (3,730 miles) of the Moon's surface in January 1959.

• The first successful fly-by mission outside the Earth-Moon system was the Mariner 2 probe which passed Venus at a distance of about 35,000 km (21,750 miles) in December 1962.

# LANDERS

SPACE PROBES SENT to orbit a planet can release a second craft to land on the surface. The lander, a scientific robot, carries out its preprogrammed tasks and then relays the data it has obtained back to Earth. So far, landers have provided information about the Moon, Venus, and Mars.

COMING IN TO LAND
This dramatic photograph of lunar craters was taken from one of the Apollo landers during its low-altitude descent to the Moon's surface.

IS THERE LIFE ON MARS?
Two Viking orbiter craft each released a lander that descended safely to the Martian surface. In total about 3,000 photographic images were sent back to Earth. The landers also tested the Martian soil with four different experiments to check for any signs of life – none was found.

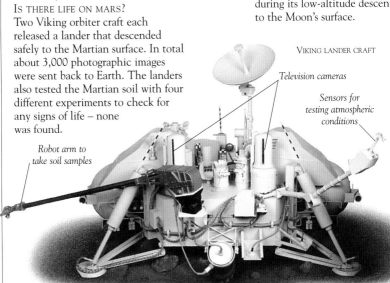

VIKING LANDER CRAFT

*Television cameras*

*Sensors for testing atmospheric conditions*

*Robot arm to take soil samples*

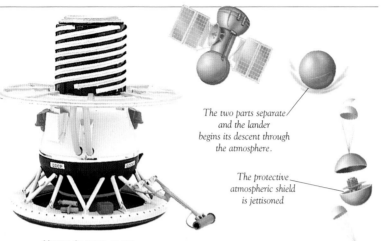

*The two parts separate and the lander begins its descent through the atmosphere.*

*The protective atmospheric shield is jettisoned*

VENERA 9 LANDER CRAFT

*On-board braking engines begin to slow Venera 9*

### LANDER FACTS

• The first successful lander was Luna 9, which soft-landed on the Moon in 1966.

• Venera 7 became the first lander to transmit data from the surface of Venus in 1970.

• The Viking landers analysed Mars' soil and found that it contained the following chemical elements:

| | |
|---|---|
| silica | 14% |
| iron | 18% |
| aluminum | 2.7% |
| titanium | 0.9% |
| potassium | 0.3% |

### HOT LANDING

A series of Venera space probes was sent to Venus. Each consisted of two parts, one of which descended to the surface. Conditions on Venus – very high temperature and pressure – meant that the landers could function only for a few minutes.

*Parachutes further slow the descent*

*Venera 9 obtains and transmits several images before failing*

# WORKING IN SPACE

ASTRONAUTS NOW WORK in space on a regular basis. Many experiments are carried out aboard orbiting laboratories; and satellites are launched, retrieved, and repaired while in Earth orbit.

WORKING ON THE MOON
Buzz Aldrin (the second man to walk on the Moon) sets up one of the scientific experiment packages that the Apollo 11 crew left behind on the lunar surface.

*Steering control*

*Television camera*

*Equipment storage rack*

*Antenna*

*Wire-mesh wheels*

LUNAR ROVING VEHICLE (LRV)

MOON BUGGY
Crew members of the Apollo 15, 16, and 17 missions made effective use of the LRV. This "moon-buggy" enabled them to travel tens of miles (kilometers) across the lunar surface collecting samples over a wide area.

SELF-PROPELLED
Powered by small jets of nitrogen gas, the Manned Maneuvering Unit enables astronauts to move about freely outside their spacecraft.

MANNED MANEUVERING UNIT

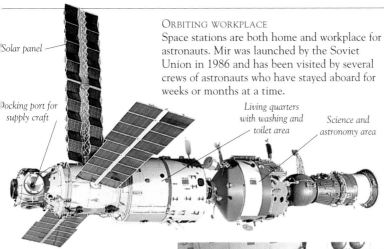

Solar panel

Docking port for
supply craft

*Living quarters
with washing and
toilet area*

*Science and
astronomy area*

### ORBITING WORKPLACE
Space stations are both home and workplace for astronauts. Mir was launched by the Soviet Union in 1986 and has been visited by several crews of astronauts who have stayed aboard for weeks or months at a time.

### LABORATORY CONDITIONS
A crew member places a specimen inside one of the zero-gravity experiment chambers located in the Space Shuttle's crew compartment. Larger scale experiments can be carried out in the cargo bay using computer-controlled equipment.

### RUNNING REPAIRS
The Space Shuttle lets astronauts position themselves alongside a faulty satellite and either repair it in space, or bring it back to Earth for overhaul. The most successful repair mission to date was in December 1993, when new optical equipment was installed on the Hubble Space Telescope.

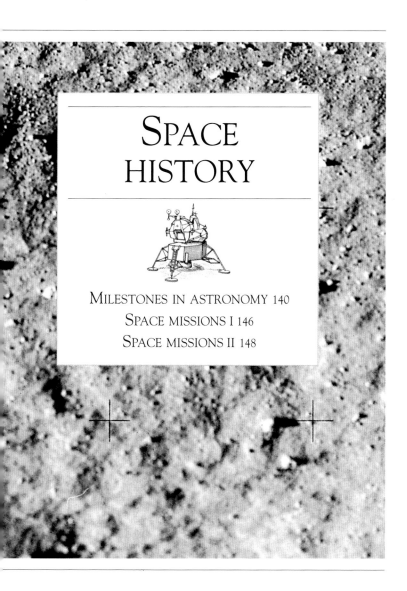

# SPACE HISTORY

# MILESTONES IN ASTRONOMY

The astronomer's job is to observe, describe, and explain objects in space. The story of astronomy is marked by a series of milestone achievements. Advances in technology have led to better descriptions and more comprehensive explanations.

EUDOXUS OF CNIDUS (408-355 B.C.) was a Greek thinker who studied at Athens under the philosopher Plato. In later life he developed the theory of crystal spheres – the first scientific attempt to explain the observed motion of the planets, and stars.

MILESTONE
According to Eudoxus, the Earth was at the center of the universe. The stars and planets were set into a series of transparent crystal spheres that surrounded the Earth in space.

PTOLEMY (c.A.D. 120-180) lived in Alexandria, Egypt, at the height of the Roman Empire. Although little is known about him, he has become famous as the "father of astronomy." The idea that the Earth is at the center of the universe is often referred to as the "Ptolemaic System."

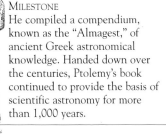

MILESTONE
He compiled a compendium, known as the "Almagest," of ancient Greek astronomical knowledge. Handed down over the centuries, Ptolemy's book continued to provide the basis of scientific astronomy for more than 1,000 years.

AL-SUFI (903-86) was a Persian nobleman, and one of the leading astronomers of his time. His "Book of Fixed Stars" listed the position and brightness of more than 1,000 stars, and beautifully illustrated the main constellations.

MILESTONE
During the Dark Ages, scientific astronomy was kept alive in the Islamic empire. Our knowledge of the works of Ptolemy is entirely due to Arab translators.

NICOLAUS COPERNICUS (1473-1543) worked as a church lawyer in Poland. Near the end of his life he published an exciting new view of the universe which replaced Ptolemy's.

MILESTONE
Copernicus removed the Earth from its traditional place at the center of the universe, and replaced it with the Sun. This was considered to be revolutionary view, and the "Copernican Revolution" was strongly opposed by the Christian Church.

GALILEO GALILEI (1564-1642) was an Italian scientist and astronomer who supported Copernicus' new theory. As a result, he was put on trial by the Church, and he remained a virtual prisoner for the rest of his life.

MILESTONE
Galileo pioneered the use of the refractor telescope for astronomy. He made several major discoveries, including mountains on the Moon, the phases of Venus, and the four largest moons of Jupiter.

ISAAC NEWTON (1643-1727) was a professor of mathematics and a great scientist. He is supposed to have had the idea for his theory of gravity after seeing an apple fall from a tree.

MILESTONE
The theory of gravity explained why apples fall, and why planets orbit around the Sun. Newton was able to establish the scientific laws that apply to the motion of objects in space. He also experimented with optics – splitting sunlight into its spectrum – and designed a reflecting telescope.

EDMOND HALLEY (1656-1742) became Britain's Astronomer Royal – one of the first official government scientists. As a young man he voyaged to the remote island of St. Helena, and charted the stars of the Southern Hemisphere.

MILESTONE
Halley is famous for predicting the return of the periodic comet that now bears his name. His work reinforced the idea that astronomy is a very precise science that can make accurate predictions.

WILLIAM HERSCHEL (1738-1822) was born in Hanover, Germany, but moved to England where he at first worked as a professional musician. His interest in astronomy led him to design and build his own telescopes.

MILESTONE
Herschel became famous for his discovery of the planet Uranus in 1781. Today he is remembered as one of the greatest astronomical observers. By studying the Milky Way over many years, he was able to make the first reasonably accurate estimate of its size and shape.

JOSEPH VON FRAUNHOFER (1787-1826) was an orphan who eventually became the director of a scientific institute in Germany. He was a trained optical worker who made some of the world's highest-quality telescope lenses.

MILESTONE
Fraunhofer identified and studied the dark absorption lines (now called Fraunhofer lines) in the solar spectrum. These lines enable scientists to tell which chemical elements are present in a source of light.

NEPTUNE (FIRST LOCATED IN 1846) The position of a new planet in the solar system was predicted mathematically. But its existence could not be confirmed until it had been observed.

MILESTONE
The "discovery" of Neptune was made possible by astronomers' increased understanding of the universe. Following the work of Newton and Halley, they were able to make increasingly accurate predictions about the behavior of objects in space.

WILLIAM HUGGINS (1824-1910) was an English astronomer who had his own private observatory in London. He was a pioneer of the technique of stellar spectroscopy (analysing the spectra produced by starlight).

MILESTONE
Huggins studied the light from many different stars. As a result of his work, he was able to show that stars are made of the same chemical elements that are found on Earth. He also showed that some nebulae are composed of gas.

GIOVANNI SCHIAPARELLI (1835-1910) was an Italian astronomer who became director of the Brera Observatory at Turin. He made headlines in 1877, when he claimed to be able to see a network of canals on Mars.

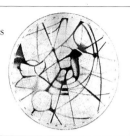

MILESTONE
Schiaparelli's most famous discovery was mistaken, but it did focus popular interest and attention on astronomy. He also established the link between comets and meteor showers.

EJNAR HERTZSPRUNG (1873-1967) and HENRY RUSSELL (1877-1957) were two scientists who, working independently, came to the same conclusions about the color and temperature of stars.

MILESTONE
The Hertzsprung-Russell (HR) diagram shows the relationship between surface temperature and color. Astronomers can identify the so-called "main sequence" of stellar development. Giant, supergiant, and dwarf stars are also located on the diagram.

ARTHUR EDDINGTON (1882-1945) was born in the north of England and became Professor of Astronomy at Cambridge. He was interested in the origin of stars, and he wrote science books for a general audience.

MILESTONE
Eddington was able to describe the structure of a star. He also explained how a star stays in one piece – balanced by the forces of gravity (pulling in), and gas pressure and radiation pressure (pushing out).

HARLOW SHAPLEY (1885-1972) was an American astronomer who became director of Harvard College Observatory. He used various stars as markers to study the distance and distribution of star clusters.

MILESTONE
Shapley was able to give the first accurate estimate of the size and shape of the Milky Way galaxy. He also showed that the Sun is located a very long way from the center of the galaxy.

CECILIA PAYNE-GAPOSCHKIN (1900-79) was born in England, but spent most of her working life at Harvard Observatory in the US. She is thought by many people to have been the greatest ever woman astronomer.

MILESTONE
By analysing the spectra of many different stars, Payne-Gaposchkin was able to show that all stars in the main sequence of development (the Sun for example) are composed almost entirely of the chemical elements hydrogen and helium.

EDWIN HUBBLE (1889-1953) was an American who began his working life as a lawyer before becoming a professional astronomer. He showed that the Andromeda spiral was definitely not part of the Milky Way galaxy.

MILESTONE
By showing that some objects are located outside the Milky Way, Hubble proved the existence of other galaxies. He also discovered that the universe appears to be constantly expanding.

GEORGES LEMAITRE (1894-1966) was a Belgian mathematician who worked in Britain and the US. His work had an important influence on the way that astronomers think about the universe.

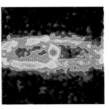

MILESTONE
Lemaître proposed and developed the Big Bang theory about the origin of the universe. According to this theory, all matter and energy were created simultaneously by a huge explosion. This theory explains why many galaxies appear to be speeding away from us.

KARL JANSKY (1905-49) was an American radio engineer. While trying to solve the problem of static and interference with radio broadcasts, he discovered radio waves coming from the Milky Way.

MILESTONE
Without realizing it, Jansky discovered the basic techniques of radio astronomy. As a result of his work, astronomers have been able to to gather information from other parts of the electromagnetic spectrum, and not just from visible light.

FRED HOYLE (b. 1915) is a British astronomer who began his career as a mathematician. He became famous for his theory that life on Earth was the result of infection by bacteria from space carried by comets.

MILESTONE
Hoyle's most important work concerned the basic nuclear reactions at work deep inside stars. He explained the processes by which stars convert hydrogen into helium and other heavier elements.

FRED WHIPPLE (b. 1906) was appointed professor of astronomy at Harvard in 1945, and became director of the Smithsonian Astrophysical Observatory in 1955. He is best known for his studies of comets and the solar system.

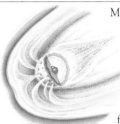

MILESTONE
His theory that comets are "dirty snowballs" has recently been proved correct by space probes such as Giotto. It now seems likely that comets are "leftovers" from the formation of the solar system.

ARNO PENZIAS (b. 1933) AND ROBERT WILSON (b. 1936) are American scientists. In 1978 they received the Nobel prize for physics for discovering the background radio energy of the universe – energy that is left over from the Big Bang.

MILESTONE
This radio energy ("the microwave background") gives the universe an average temperature about 5°F (3°C) above absolute zero. Many people believe that its discovery confirmed the Big Bang theory.

SUPERNOVA 1987A The observation of a bright supernova during 1987 gave astronomers their first opportunity to study a supernova event with modern telescopes and other equipment.

MILESTONE
Analysis of the energy and particles produced by the event confirmed the theory that all chemical elements heavier than iron are made by very high-temperature nuclear reactions during supernova explosions.

# SPACE MISSIONS I

THE SPACE AGE began in 1957 with the launch of the first satellite. Four years later Yuri Gagarin became the world's first astronaut. The next 20 years saw a surge of interest in space exploration.

FIRST SPACE VEHICLE
A model of Vostok I, the craft in which Yuri Gagarin made his historic first orbit o the Earth on April 12, 1961.

CONTROLLED LANDING
The probe Luna 9 was the first to make a successful soft landing on the Moon in February 1966. Luna 9 sent back the first panoramic images taken from the surface of the Moon.

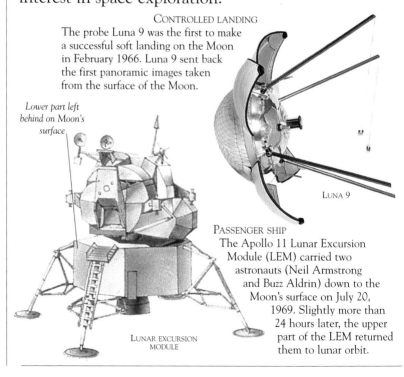

*Lower part left behind on Moon's surface*

LUNA 9

PASSENGER SHIP
The Apollo 11 Lunar Excursion Module (LEM) carried two astronauts (Neil Armstrong and Buzz Aldrin) down to the Moon's surface on July 20, 1969. Slightly more than 24 hours later, the upper part of the LEM returned them to lunar orbit.

LUNAR EXCURSION MODULE

## ROBOT MOON ROVER
Two Lunokhod robot vehicles were sent to the Moon in the early 1970s. Equipped with television cameras that enabled them to be driven from a control room on Earth, the two vehicles traveled a total of 29.5 miles (47.5 km) across the Moon.

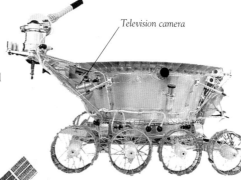

*Television camera*

LUNOKHOD I

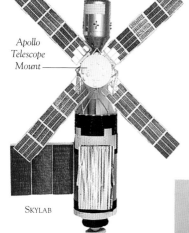

*Apollo Telescope Mount*

SKYLAB

## SCIENTIFIC PLATFORM
Launched in 1973, the Skylab orbiting laboratory and observatory gave astronauts the opportunity to work in space for weeks at a time. Skylab also enabled scientists to study the workings of Earth's atmosphere and climate systems from the viewpoint of space.

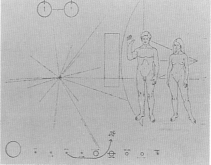

## MESSAGE TO THE STARS
The two Pioneer probes each carry a gold-covered plaque that shows a visual representation of human beings, as well as simple directions for locating the solar system and planet Earth.

# SPACE MISSIONS II

WORKING IN ORBIT became much easier with the introduction of the Space Shuttle in 1981. Probes have now visited all but one of the outer planets, and further exploration is planned.

*The Shuttle has a mechanical arm which can be used to launch or retrieve satellites.*

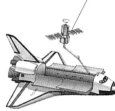

*The external fuel tank breaks away at a height of 70 miles (110 km)*

*The booster rockets operate for about two minutes and are jettisoned at a height of 28 miles (45 km).*

*The Shuttle can lift off with eight crew and up to 29 tons (tonnes) of cargo.*

INCREASING COMMUNICATIONS
The communications satellite Intelsat was launched by astronauts on the 49th Space Shuttle mission in May 1992. Improved communications is just one of the benefits of space technology now enjoyed by the general public.

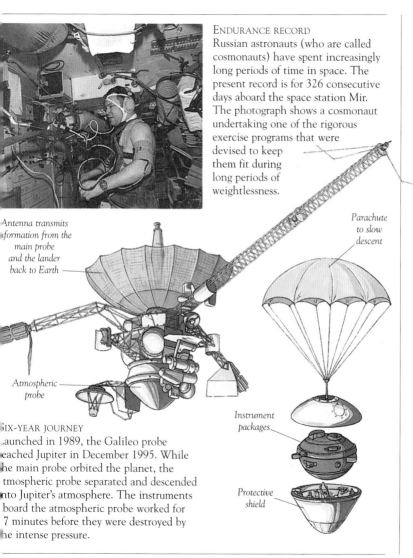

ENDURANCE RECORD

Russian astronauts (who are called cosmonauts) have spent increasingly long periods of time in space. The present record is for 326 consecutive days aboard the space station Mir. The photograph shows a cosmonaut undertaking one of the rigorous exercise programs that were devised to keep them fit during long periods of weightlessness.

Antenna transmits information from the main probe and the lander back to Earth

Parachute to slow descent

Atmospheric probe

Instrument packages

Protective shield

SIX-YEAR JOURNEY

Launched in 1989, the Galileo probe reached Jupiter in December 1995. While the main probe orbited the planet, the atmospheric probe separated and descended into Jupiter's atmosphere. The instruments aboard the atmospheric probe worked for 57 minutes before they were destroyed by the intense pressure.

149

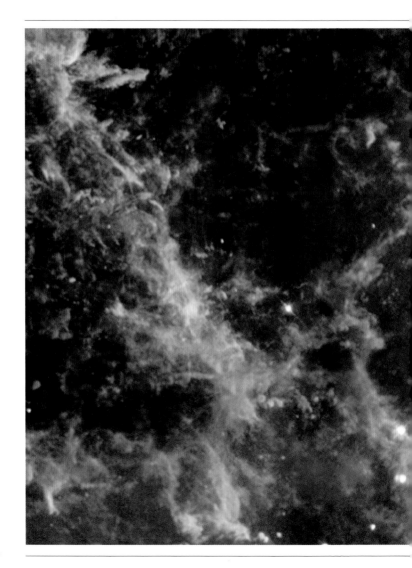

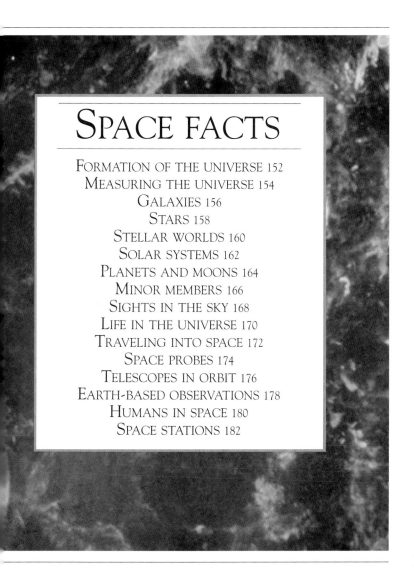

# SPACE FACTS

# FORMATION OF THE UNIVERSE

## IN THE BEGINNING...

- The universe – that's everything, all time, space, and matter – was created about 13 billion years ago.

- An explosion, which scientists have named the Big Bang, produced the universe which at birth was a hot mass of tiny particles.

- For about the first quarter of a million years of its life, the universe was a "soup" of mainly hydrogen and helium.

- By the time the universe was one billion years old, its material was being pulled into clouds. The first stars were about to be born.

## PROFILE OF THE UNIVERSE

**DEFINITION** – everything that exists

**AGE** – about 13 billion years

**COMPOSITION** – mainly hydrogen and helium

**MOST DISTANT OBJECTS VISIBLE** – about 10 billion light years away

**AVERAGE TEMPERATURE** – -454°F (-270°C )

**NUMBER OF GALAXIES** – 100 billion

**KNOWN LIFE** – 6 billion humans, plus other uncountable life forms, all on Earth

## FOUR FORCES

The very young universe was controlled by one "superforce". As the universe expanded and cooled, the superforce split into four separate forces – gravity, a "strong" force, a "weak" force, and an electromagnetic force. Gravity keeps objects in orbit, the strong force keeps the nuclei of atoms together, the weak force governs how the stars shine, and the electromagnetic force controls electricity and magnetism.

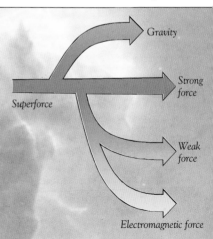

Gravity

Strong force

Superforce

Weak force

Electromagnetic force

## STAR NURSERY

New stars are being born all the time. This picture shows young, hot, bright stars lighting up the gas and material surrounding them. These are in a nearby spiral galaxy, but nurseries of stars such as this one exist in galaxies throughout the universe.

## THE CHANGING UNIVERSE

- The universe is always changing. All of the objects within it are part of a continuing cycle of birth, death, and rebirth. It is also expanding.

- We call the rate of expansion Hubble's Constant, after Edwin Hubble, the astronomer who calculated the rate.

- The further that a galaxy is from us, the faster it is moving away. The view is the same from other galaxies, every galaxy is moving away from every other one.

- The material of the universe is being constantly recycled. The remains of old stars are used to make new stars.

- Simple elements, such as hydrogen and helium, are transformed inside stars into more complex elements, such as carbon, oxygen, and iron.

## THE UNKNOWN UNIVERSE

- Astronomers have detected only a small part of the material in the universe.

- The universe's unknown material is called dark matter. It is believed to make up about 95% of the total matter of the universe.

- Dark matter is known to exist because we can see the effect of its gravity on those parts of the universe that we can detect.

- Some dark matter may be in the form of planet-sized objects found in the spherical regions (haloes) around spiral galaxies.

- Most dark matter is thought to consist of tiny subatomic particles.

153

# MEASURING THE UNIVERSE

## MEASURING METHODS

Different measuring methods and units are used for different objects in the Universe.

- Astronomers can measure the distance to the Moon by reflecting a laser beam back to Earth from the lunar surface.

- By measuring the amount of time it takes a radar signal to be bounced back from the Sun and nearby planets, astronomers can calculate their distance from Earth.

- The parallax method is used to measure the distance of nearby stars. Astronomers record the position of a star twice – at opposite ends of the Earth's orbit of the Sun. The parallax is the apparent shift in position of the star against the background of more distant stars. The greater the parallax, the nearer the star.

- The distance to a nearby galaxy is found by studying the brightness of Cepheid (regularly pulsating) stars within the galaxy.

- The distance to a remote galaxy is found by comparing its properties with those of a galaxy of known distance.

### DEEP SPACE VIEW

Nearly every dot, smudge and speck of light in this photograph is a galaxy, each one containing billions of stars. Some of the galaxies are so distant, we see them as they were 10 billion years ago, when they were very young.

## SIZE OF OBJECTS IN THE UNIVERSE

| OBJECT | DIAMETER |
| --- | --- |
| Eros (asteroid) | 33 km (20.5 miles) |
| Earth | 12,756 km (7,926 miles) |
| Sun | 1.4 million km (869,920 miles) |
| Solar System | 1.6 light years |
| Milky Way Galaxy | 100,000 light years |
| Local group of galaxies | 5 million light years |
| Local supercluster of galaxies | 120 million light years |

## DISTANCE FROM EARTH TO OBJECTS IN THE UNIVERSE

| OBJECT | DISTANCE FROM EARTH |
| --- | --- |
| Moon | 384,400 km (238,855 miles) |
| Sun | 149.6 million km (93 million miles) |
| Alpha Centauri | 4.4 light years |
| Orion Nebula | 1600 light years |
| Andromeda Galaxy | 2,500,000 light years |
| Coma Cluster of galaxies | 290 million light years |
| Quasar 3C 273 | 2,100 million light years |
| Radio galaxy 3C 368 | 8,400 million light years |
| The most distant detected objects | around 10,000 million light years |

## THE MOVING UNIVERSE

Everything in the Universe is always moving. Objects spin, orbit other objects, and travel across space.

- Earth spins on its axis, orbits around the Sun, and, as part of the Solar System, moves round the Milky Way. The Milky Way is moving through space.

- Some objects, such as pulsars (spinning neutron stars), spin incredibly quickly, many hundreds of times a second.

  Venus spins on its axis only once in 243 days – less than the time it takes to orbit the Sun.

- Six planets, including Earth, spin in the same direction as they orbit the Sun. Uranus is tilted on its side; Venus and Pluto turn backwards.

- Spin rates and orbits change. Earth's spin rate is decreasing and the Moon is gradually moving away from Earth.

### SPINNING SUN

The Sun, like all other objects in the Universe, spins. But because it is a sphere of gas and not solid, it does not spin at one speed. Its equator rotates once in about 25 days; while near the poles, it makes one rotation every 35 days.

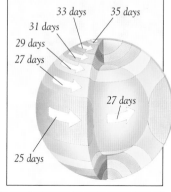

155

# GALAXIES

## EVOLUTION OF GALAXIES

- All galaxies, including the Milky Way, started life as a vast cloud of gas.

- A galaxy begins to form when the gas cloud shrinks, the gas becomes more dense and starts to form stars. At the same time, the galaxy starts to spin.

- The spin speed, the amount of material, and the birth rate of a galaxy's stars all help to determine the shape of the galaxy.

- Ball-shaped, or egg-shaped galaxies are called ellipticals. A spiral galaxy has distinctive "arms" extending from its center.

- Galaxies are found in clusters. It is not certain whether galaxies form in clusters or gather into clusters after formation.

*In this spiral galaxy, NGC 4414, the older yellow and red stars are in the center. The arms are rich in young blue stars, bright nebulae, and interstellar gas and dust.*

## MILKY WAY GALAXY

- Our galaxy's center contains millions of stars, more densely packed than anywhere else in the galaxy.

- There is believed to be a giant black hole at the heart of our galaxy. It is 2.5 to 3 million times the mass of the Sun.

- Two other galaxies – the Large and the Small Magellanic Clouds – orbit the Milky Way on elliptical paths.

- The Milky Way's gravity is pulling at the Small Magellanic Cloud. Its stars will eventually end up as part of our galaxy.

# ACTIVE GALAXIES

- A small number of galaxies are different from the rest – they pour out huge amounts of energy from their centers. These are known as active galaxies.

- At the center of an active galaxy is a very luminous core containing a massive black hole. Two huge jets of material shoot out from its center.

- Quasars, blazars, Seyfert galaxies, and radio galaxies are all types of active galaxies.

- All active galaxies share similar properties and some astronomers believe that there may only be one type. They think the different "types" depend on the galaxy's distance and the angle that it appears in our sky.

## INTERACTING GALAXIES

- A collision between two relatively slow-moving galaxies can produce a new one with a different shape. Fast-moving galaxies can pass through each other completely.

- In a galactic collision, giant clouds of gas in the galaxies crash together, resulting in the production of lots of new stars.

- Gravity is pulling the Milky Way and Andromeda galaxies together. It is thought eventually they, and other smaller galaxies, will merge.

- The Cartwheel Galaxy was once a normal spiral galaxy, but a smaller galaxy moved through it about 300 million years ago, creating the wheel shape of today.

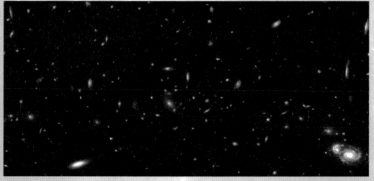

*At least a dozen galaxies in this galactic cluster are colliding to form new, more massive galaxies.*

GALAXIES

157

## THE BRIGHTEST STARS IN THE SKY

Star brightness is measured in magnitudes. The smaller the magnitude number, the brighter the star – the brightest have negative magnitudes. These are the brightest stars in the night sky.

| STAR | CONSTELLATION | MAGNITUDE |
|------|--------------|-----------|
| Sirius | Canis Major | -1.46 |
| Canopus | Carina | -0.6 |
| Rigil Kentaurus | Centaurus | -0.27 |
| Arcturus | Boötes | -0.04 |
| Vega | Lyra | 0.03 |
| Capella | Auriga | 0.08 |
| Rigel | Orion | 0.12 |
| Procyon | Canis Minor | 0.38 |
| Achernar | Eridanus | 0.46 |
| Betelgeuse | Orion | 0.50 |
| Hadar | Centaurus | 0.61 |
| Acrux | Crux | 0.76 |
| Altair | Aquila | 0.77 |
| Aldebaran | Taurus | 0.85 |

## OUR OWN STAR

The Sun is the only star we can study in close-up. It is a violent place, which periodically erupts and expels huge streams of glowing gas from its surface. Such bursts can be many thousands of miles long.

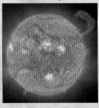

## STAR MASS AND SIZE

Astronomers are interested in the mass of a star – that's the amount of material it is made of. They describe stars in solar masses; so a star of 60 solar masses is made of 60 times the material in the Sun.

- There are many more small stars than massive ones.

- The smallest star type, brown dwarves, have less than 0.08 solar mass, that's only about 75 or 80 Jupiters.

- The most massive stars are 60-120 solar masses.

- A red giant is 30 times the size of the Sun, and the Sun is 100 times the size of a white dwarf.

- The very largest stars have diameters that are 300 times bigger than that of the Sun.

- Neutron stars are the size of a large city, like New York, but weigh as much as several Suns.

- In the late 1990s, astronomers detected a new class of small star, so far unnamed, that is only as massive as 10-20 Jupiters.

## BETWEEN THE STARS

The space between the stars contains gas and dust used in star formation.

- Compared to even the thinnest part of Earth's atmosphere, the space between the stars is incredibly empty. However, it is not a vacuum.

- A typical matchbox-sized volume of interstellar space contains about half a dozen hydrogen atoms and a grain or two of dust.

- Interstellar material makes up one-tenth of the Milky Way Galaxy.

- Material between the stars is in constant change. It is used in the formation of stars and is replaced by new material from dying stars.

- About half of the interstellar material is in molecular clouds, and about half is in the space between the clouds.

- Molecular clouds are dark, dense volumes of molecules of gas and dust which give birth to stars.

*The Cygnus Loop is one of the hottest but least dense parts of interstellar material.*

## GIANTS AND SUPERGIANTS

These are the names, colors, and locations of the giant and supergiant stars.

| STAR NAME | CONSTELLATION | STAR COLOR |
| --- | --- | --- |
| GIANTS | | |
| Arcturus | Boötes | Orange |
| Capella | Auriga | Yellow |
| Hadar | Centaurus | Blue |
| Aldebaran | Taurus | Red |
| Pollux | Gemini | Orange |
| SUPERGIANTS | | |
| Canopus | Carina | White |
| Rigel | Orion | Blue |
| Betelgeuse | Orion | Red |
| Antares | Scorpius | Red |
| Deneb | Cygnus | White |

## SOME BIRTHPLACES OF STARS

Stars are born in a vast, glowing cloud of dust called a nebula. These are four of the biggest and best-known nebulas, along with their distances from Earth.

| NEBULA | CONSTELLATION | DISTANCE IN LIGHT YEARS |
|--------|---------------|-------------------------|
| Orion | Orion | 1600 |
| Omega | Sagittarius | 5000 |
| Lagoon | Sagittarius | 5200 |
| Eagle | Serpens | 7000 |

### STAR FAMILIES

- Stars are always born as part of a group, from a nebula of gas and dust.

- Open clusters – families of young stars – can be made up of any amount, from 10 to several thousand stars.

- About half of all stars are twins, triplets, or groups of four or more. These are called multiple star systems.

- Some stars are so close together that they share an outer atmosphere, or pass gas between them.

- Globular clusters are tightly knit swarms of thousands or millions of older stars.

*Stars are forming within these pillarlike structures of the Eagle Nebula in the constellation Serpens.*

## EXPLODING STARS

- Stars can explode at any point during their lifetime.

- Some newly-formed, massive stars explode and produce huge bursts of gamma rays.

- Some stars brighten then fade as they undergo eruptive change.

- A nova is a bright star, produced suddenly when a white dwarf pulls hydrogen off its binary companion, leading to an enormous explosion.

- The most massive stars end their lives in a colossal explosion known as a supernova. Around two or three supernovas are expected to occur in our galaxy each century.

- Supernova 1987A was the first supernova explosion in a galaxy near Earth since 1604.

## CHANGING STARS

- When a star's supply of hydrogen runs out, it burns helium and becomes a red giant, puffing off its outer layers of gas as it matures.

- A mature star enveloped by clouds of expelled gas is called a planetary nebula.

- The shape made by a planetary nebula's gas gives it its name. Examples include Dumbbell, Cat's Eye, Ring, and Butterfly.

- Stars often pulsate, making them vary in brightness, temperature, and size as they near the end of their life.

- The Sun will become a type of pulsating star, a Cepheid variable. It will constantly shrink and expand before turning into a white dwarf.

### ANCIENT CLUSTER

This photograph shows hundreds of thousands of stars, packed together in this ancient globular cluster. Scientists estimate that there are about 200 such clusters in the Milky Way Galaxy – 140 have been identified so far. Globular cluster stars are among the oldest in the Galaxy and are typically 10 billion years old.

# SOLAR SYSTEMS

## FORMATION OF OUR SOLAR SYSTEM

- The solar system – the Sun and its orbiting planets – was created 4,600 million years ago from a large cloud of gas and dust called the solar nebula.

- The Sun formed in the center of the solar nebula. The tiny particles of material surrounding it bumped and stuck together, forming bigger and bigger lumps to eventually create the planets.

- Each of the planets took a different length of time to form. The rocky planets (Mercury, Venus, Earth, and Mars) were formed first.

- Jupiter, Saturn, Uranus, and Neptune formed from rock, metal, snow, and gas. They first made a solid core, then captured vast atmospheres. For this reason, they are known as the "gas giants."

- Pluto, moons, asteroids, and comets were formed from the remaining material.

### IS PLUTO A PLANET?

Since its discovery, Pluto has always been regarded as a planet. However, recent observations have led some astronomers to classify it as the biggest member of a group of icy objects that lie beyond the orbit of Neptune. In this picture, Pluto's moon, Charon, is seen on the right.

## PLANETARY FORMATION

The planets are listed below in order of the time it is thought that they took to form. As a rule, the length of the formation period increases with the planet's distance from the Sun.

| PLANET | MASS (EARTH = 1) | TIME TO FORM (YEARS) |
|---|---|---|
| **1** Venus | 0.82 | 40,000 |
| **2** Mercury | 0.06 | 80,000 |
| **3** Earth | 1.00 | 110,000 |
| **4** Mars | 0.11 | 200,000 |
| **5** Jupiter | 318 | 1 million |
| **6** Saturn | 95.16 | 9 million |
| **7** Uranus | 14.54 | 300 million |
| **8** Neptune | 17.15 | 1 billion |
| **9** Pluto | 0.002 | 1 billion |

## OTHER SOLAR SYSTEMS

Extrasolar planets – those that orbit stars other than the Sun – are too distant and too small to be seen directly. However, by analyzing the behavior of a star, astronomers can work out if a planet is orbiting it.

- It is believed that one in every 25 stars has planets orbiting it.

- The Infrared Astronomical Satellite (IRAS) detected a disc of gas and dust around Beta Pictoris in 1984. This was the first evidence of planetary formation around another star.

- The first extrasolar planet was identified by the "wobble" of its star. The gravity of the massive planet made the star wobble.

- The smallest detectable planets (at present) have the same mass as Saturn.

- All the extrasolar giant planets found so far are closer to their stars than Jupiter is to the Sun.

*Perhaps it is only a matter of time before an extrasolar Earthlike planet is discovered.*

## EXTRASOLAR PLANETS

Since 1995, astronomers using highly sensitive instruments have discovered a number of extrasolar planets. The first 10 to be identified are listed below.

| | PARENT STAR | MINIMUM MASS OF PLANET (EARTH = 1) | YEAR OF DISCOVERY |
|---|---|---|---|
| 1 | 51 Pegasi | 150 | 1995 |
| 2 | 55 Cancri | 270 | 1996 |
| 3 | 47 Ursae Majoris | 890 | 1996 |
| 4 | Tau Boötis | 1230 | 1996 |
| 5 | Upsilon Andromedae | 220 | 1996 |
| 6 | 70 Virginis | 2100 | 1996 |
| 7 | 16 Cygni B | 480 | 1996 |
| 8 | Rho Coronae Borealis | 350 | 1997 |
| 9 | Gliese 876 | 670 | 1998 |
| 10 | 14 Herculis | 1050 | 1998 |

## PLANETARY FEATURES

Each of the planets in our solar system has very distinctive features.

- Of the nine planets in the solar system, four have rings and seven have moons.

- More than 75% of Venus's surface is volcanic. It has 150 volcanoes that measure more than 62 miles (100 km) across.

- At 372 miles (600 km) across, the extinct Martian volcano *Olympus Mons* is the largest in the solar system.

- Jupiter has great internal heat. It radiates twice as much heat as it receives from the Sun.

- Saturn's rings are made of almost pure ice: there is only one part of dust for every 100 million parts of ice.

## ATMOSPHERES

- The main ingredients of Venus's atmosphere are the same as the Earth's. However, they are found in significantly different proportions.

- Venus's atmosphere is so thick that only 2% of the Sun's light reaches its surface.

- The dust in Mars's atmosphere makes the daytime sky a dusty-pink color.

- Jupiter and Saturn have giant storms in their atmospheres. The biggest is the Great Red Spot on Jupiter, a giant hurricane that has lasted for over 300 years.

- Pluto has an atmosphere that comes and goes. When closest to the Sun, some of its ice turns to gas. This gas freezes back to ice when the planet moves further away.

*This is the crater of the Martian volcano Apollinaris Patera. It is 50 miles (80 km) across.*

## AURORAE ON JUPITER

This photograph shows colouful aurorae above Jupiter's polar regions. These are solar particles, which are drawn toward the poles and interact with the planet's atmosphere. Earth's northern and southern lights look much the same when seen from space.

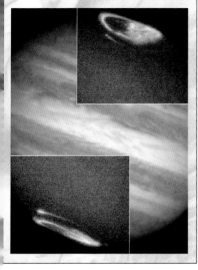

## MOONS

Mercury and Venus are the only planets in our solar system without moons. The others have moons that vary greatly in size and composition.

- Around 100 moons are known to orbit the planets in our solar system. Astronomers believe there are more small ones waiting to be discovered.

- The first to be discovered, apart from the Earth's Moon, were the four largest moons of Jupiter, in 1610.

- Jupiter's moon *Io* is the most volcanically active body in the solar system. It is believed to have about 300 active volcanoes.

- Saturn's Titan is the only moon with a thick atmosphere. It is rich in nitrogen and orange in color.

- The surface of *Triton*, Neptune's largest moon, has been shaped by ice volcanism. It has lakes of ice lava more than 62 miles (100 km) across.

## LARGEST MOONS

These are the five biggest moons in our solar system. The largest two – Ganymede and Titan – are bigger than Pluto and Mercury, the two smallest planets.

| MOON | PARENT PLANET | DIAMETER |
|------|---------------|----------|
| **1** Ganymede | Jupiter | 3,269 miles (5,262 km) |
| **2** Titan | Saturn | 3,200 miles (5,150 km) |
| **3** Callisto | Jupiter | 2,982 miles (4,800 km) |
| **4** Io | Jupiter | 2,255 miles (3,630 km) |
| **5** Moon | Earth | 2,160 miles (3,476 km) |

# MINOR MEMBERS OF THE SOLAR SYSTEM

## ASTEROIDS

- Asteroids are chunks of space rock orbiting the Sun. They are sometimes called minor planets.

- They are made of rock, metal, or a combination of both.

- Only those over about 186 miles (300 km) across are spherical. Most asteroids are irregular in shape.

- More than 90% of asteroids orbit the Sun in the Asteroid Belt, or Main Belt, which lies between the orbits of Mars and Jupiter.

- The Apollo, Amor, and Aten groups of asteroids lie outside the Main Belt. Their orbits bring them close to the Earth's orbit.

*The asteroid Ida has its own moon, Dactyl (pictured right).*

## COMETS

- A comet is a lump of snow and rocky dust that follows its own orbit around the Sun.

- Around 10 trillion comets exist in the Oort Cloud, a spherical cloud that surrounds the planetary solar system. Occasionally, a comet leaves it and moves toward the Sun.

- As the comet nears the Sun, its nucleus (center) develops a glowing head (the coma) and two enormous tails – one of gas and one of dust.

- Once every 10 years or so, a comet is bright enough to be seen in the night sky with the naked eye. The most recent was Hale-Bopp in 1997.

## METEORS

- Bright streaks of light seen in the night sky are called meteors. They are caused by pieces of space rock, meteoroids, burning up as they enter the Earth's atmosphere.

- Due to their appearance, meteors are often called "shooting stars".

- The Earth regularly passes through large streams of meteoroids. This results in a meteor shower.

- The brightest meteors are called fireballs. They appear brighter than any star or planet. There are estimated to be tens of thousands each year.

- About 5,000 fireballs explode each year. They are called bolides.

## METEORITES

- A meteorite is a large meteoroid that survives the Earth's atmosphere and lands on the surface.

- Out of the many thousands of meteorites that land on the Earth's surface each year, about 3,000 weigh more than 2.2 lb (1 kg).

- The dark-colored rocks are easy to spot on the undisturbed areas of Earth, such as Antarctica and the desert regions of Australia and Africa. Around 10 meteorites a year are found in these places.

- A mountain-sized meteorite hit the Earth 65 million years ago and made the 124-mile (200-km) Chicxulub Crater on the coast of Mexico.

## MOON CRATER

The Moon has no atmosphere, so anything heading toward it reaches the surface. It is covered with many craters caused by the impact of meteorites of all sizes. The lack of water and weather on the Moon means that the craters remain unchanged, unless they are reshaped by further impacts.

MINOR MEMBERS

# SIGHTS IN THE SKY

## TOTAL SOLAR ECLIPSES

A total solar eclipse occurs when the Moon passes directly in front of the Sun and casts a shadow over part of the Earth. Here are the next six that you can see:

| DATE | MAXIMUM DURATION | VISIBLE FROM |
|------|------------------|--------------|
| Dec 4, 2002 | 2 mins 4 secs | Southern Africa, Indian Ocean, Australia |
| Nov 23, 2003 | 1 min 57 secs | Antarctica |
| April 8, 2005 | 42 secs | Pacific, central America |
| March 29, 2006 | 4 min 7 secs | Atlantic, northern Africa, central Asia |
| August 1, 2008 | 2 min 27 secs | Greenland, Arctic, Russia, China |
| July 22, 2009 | 6 mins 39 secs | India, China, Pacific |

### DIAMOND RING

For a few seconds on either side of "totality" (the point in a total solar eclipse when the Sun is completely covered by the Moon), sunlight shines briefly between the mountains on the edge of the Moon to produce a dazzling "diamond ring" effect.

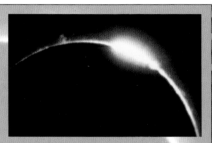

## YEARLY METEOR SHOWERS

Groups of "shooting stars" are visible in the night sky at these times each year:

| DATE | NAME | CONSTELLATION |
|------|------|---------------|
| January 1-6 | Quadrantids | Boötes |
| April 19-24 | Lyrids | Lyra |
| May 1-8 | Eta Aquarids | Aquarius |
| July 15 -August 15 | Delta Aquarids | Aquarius |
| July 25 -August 18 | Perseids | Perseus |
| October 16-27 | Orionids | Orion |
| October 20 -November 30 | Taurids | Taurus |
| November 15-20 | Leonids | Leo |
| December 7-15 | Geminids | Gemini |

# COMETARY VISITORS

Comets are only visible from Earth when they travel through the inner solar system. These will all be visible using binoculars:

| COMET | CONSTELLATION | VIEWING DATE |
|---|---|---|
| Encke | Aquila | December 2003 |
| Tempel 1 | Virgo | June 2005 |
| Chernykh | Cetus | October 2005 |
| Schwassmann-Wachmann 3 | Hercules | May 2006 |
| Honda-Mrkos-Pajdusakova | Aries | June 2006 |
| Faye | Pisces | November 2006 |
| Tuttle | Pisces | January 2008 |
| 22 Kopff | Aquarius | July 2009 |
| Wild 2 | Virgo | March 2010 |

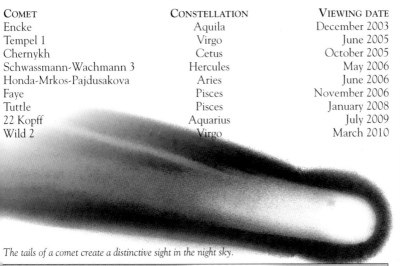

*The tails of a comet create a distinctive sight in the night sky.*

## NIGHT SKY SIGHTS

- Sunlight reflected off the panels of the *International Space Station* make it visible to the naked eye.

- Light bending around the Earth and through its atmosphere can make the Moon look red during a lunar eclipse.

- The Moon often has a faint glow soon after the New Moon. This is called "Earthshine" and is caused by light bouncing off the Earth.

- Aurorae – red, pink, green, and blue lights which are shaped into rays, streamers, and arcs often appear in the sky above the Earth's polar regions.

- Aurorae are difficult to predict and can happen at any time. On average there is a display once a month.

169

## LIFE ON EARTH

- Earth is the only place in the universe where we are certain that life exists.

- Scientists believe that life, in its simplest, cellular form existed on Earth 3.5 billion years ago.

- There are many forms of life on Earth, from primitive single-cell microbes to complex, intelligent human beings.

- Scientists are still discovering new life forms on Earth, such as the organisms found in rock deep beneath the planet's surface.

- Black smokers, jet streams of superheated water on Earth's ocean beds, provide the conditions for the planet's most primitive life forms, such as single-celled protozoa.

- Some scientists believe the first microbes didn't form on Earth but were brought to our planet on comets.

## REQUIREMENTS FOR LIFE

Scientists have identified the conditions that are essential for life.

- Life's crucial chemical elements are the CHNOPS elements – carbon, hydrogen, nitrogen, oxygen, phosphorus, and sulfur.

- An energy source, such as the Sun or a seabed vent pumping heat, provides the basis for the chemical reactions needed for life to evolve.

- All the life forms we know of need liquid water.

- A stable environment with a constant energy source allows life to thrive.

- Scientists use the "Goldilocks Test" to determine whether or not a planet can support life. It cannot be too close or too far away from its star, or it will be too hot or too cold. Like the porridge, the temperature needs to be just right!

- Two places outside the Earth are believed to have, or have had, the requirements for life. They are Mars, and the ocean below the ice crust on Europa (one of Jupiter's moons).

## LIFE ON MARS?

The possibility that life will be found on the Red Planet has fascinated people for centuries.

- In 1976, two *Viking* craft tested the Martian surface for signs of living organisms. None were found.

- Water ice exists in Martian soil, but during the planet's warmer past, liquid water flowed over its surface. Some scientists believe that life may have formed at that time.

- A meteorite from Mars, ALH84001, has been studied carefully since 1984. Most scientists do not think that it contains evidence of life.

- The British craft *Beagle 2* will test soil near the Martian equator for signs of life when it arrives there late in 2003.

### MARS MICROBES
Some scientists believe that these microscopic tube-shaped structures, found in the Martian meteorite ALH84001, are fossilized microorganisms.

### ARE WE ALONE?
Scientists around the world are scanning the skies for signs of alien life.

- The first SETI (Search for Extraterrestrial Intelligence) program was launched in 1960. SETI scientists then began listening for radio messages from space.

  - About 1000 stars within 200 light years of the Sun are targeted for potential signs of intelligent life.

  - The Arecibo radio dish in Puerto Rico is used for a total of 20 days a year to listen for life.

  - A disc on board *Voyagers 1* and 2 contains sounds of Earth, including the greeting "hello" in sixty languages, in case the probes are found by intelligent life as they continue their journey through interstellar space.

*SETI scientists use powerful radio telescopes to scan the skies for alien signals.*

# TRAVELING INTO SPACE

## FIRST LAUNCHES BY THE WORLD'S SPACE NATIONS AND AGENCIES

| NATION/AGENCY | SATELLITE/ROCKET | LAUNCH DATE |
|---|---|---|
| 1 USSR | *Sputnik 1* | October 1957 |
| 2 US | *Explorer 1* | January 1958 |
| 3 France | *Asterix 1* | November 1965 |
| 4 Japan | *Ohsumi* | February 1970 |
| 5 China | *Mao 1* | April 1970 |
| 6 UK | *Black Knight 1* | October 1971 |
| 8 European Space Agency (ESA) | *CAT* | December 1979 |
| 9 India | *Rohini 1* | July 1980 |
| 10 Israel | *Horizon 1* | September 1988 |
| 11 Iraq | Stage 3 of rocket | September 1988 |

## KEY MOMENTS IN ROCKET HISTORY

- The theory of rocket-powered space flight was developed in the 1880s by Russian scientist Konstantin Tsiolkovsky.

- The first liquid-fuel rocket was launched in 1926 by American rocket pioneer Robert Goddard. The flight lasted 2.5 seconds.

- The *Saturn V* rocket was developed to launch the *Apollo* craft that took American astronauts to the Moon.

- The first reusable space vehicle, the Space Transportation System (STS), or space shuttle, was launched in 1981.

- The United States is the only country with shuttles in service. The Soviets launched their shuttle *Buran* (only once) in November 1988.

- There are four space shuttles: *Columbia*, *Discovery*, *Atlantis*, and *Endeavour*. A fifth, *Challenger*, exploded after liftoff in January 1986.

*The space shuttle Discovery taking off.*

## LAUNCH PAD FACTS

Ariane 5 *on the launch pad.*

- Around two rockets a week are launched into space from somewhere in the world.

- Baikonur, in Kazakhstan, is the world's largest and oldest space center. It has been in regular use since 1957.

- The space shuttle spends about one month on the launch pad before it lifts off for space.

- An astronaut experiences increased gravity at liftoff. The maximum is 3 g-force, three times the gravity felt on the Earth.

- A countdown to lift off starts several hours before launch. Crews are strapped in about 2.5 hours before liftoff.

- All of the world's launch sites are situated close to the equator to benefit from the push of the Earth's spin.

- The *Ariane* family of rockets, which carry European craft, are launched from Korou in French Guiana.

# TRAVELING TIMES TO SPACE DESTINATIONS

| DESTINATION | TIME FROM EARTH | SPACECRAFT |
|---|---|---|
| 1 Earth orbit | 8.5 minutes | Space shuttle |
| 2 ISS | 1 day | Space shuttle |
| 3 Moon | 3.5 days | *Eagle, Apollo 11* |
| 4 Mercury | 5 months | *Mariner 10* |
| 5 Mars | 7 months | *Pathfinder* |
| 6 Venus | 15 months | *Magellan* |
| 7 Jupiter | 6 years 2 months | *Galileo* |
| 8 Saturn | 6 years 9 months | *Cassini* |
| 9 Uranus | 8 years 5 months | *Voyager 2* |
| 10 Neptune | 12 years | *Voyager 2* |

# SPACE PROBES

## SPACE PROBE PROFILE

A space probe is a car-sized robot craft launched by a rocket or space shuttle. It travels to a specific target and investigates it using its onboard instruments.

- A probe may fly by a target, orbit it or land on it. Some probes follow a course that involves more than one of these methods and more than one target.

- Ten to 20 scientific instruments are on board to record information.

- The probe receives instructions from Earth, but it can also follow a mission programmed into its onboard computer.

- Electric power is produced by solar panels or a nuclear generator.

- Thrusters are used to control the probe's direction.

## FIRST EXPLORERS

Space probes have explored most of the solar system. Which one went where first?

| FLY BY | | PROBE | DATE | NATION |
|---|---|---|---|---|
| **1** | Moon | *Luna 1* | 1959 | USSR |
| **2** | Sun | *Pioneer 5* | 1960 | US |
| **3** | Venus | *Venera 1* | 1961 | USSR |
| **4** | Mars | *Mariner 4* | 1965 | US |
| **5** | Asteroid Belt | *Pioneer 10* | 1973 | US |
| **6** | Jupiter | *Pioneer 10* | 1973 | US |
| **7** | Mercury | *Mariner 10* | 1974 | US |
| **8** | Saturn | *Pioneer 11* | 1979 | US |
| **9** | Uranus | *Voyager 2* | 1986 | US |
| **10** | Neptune | *Voyager 2* | 1989 | US |

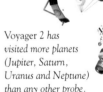

*Voyager 2 has visited more planets (Jupiter, Saturn, Uranus and Neptune) than any other probe.*

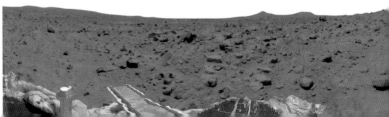

## SPACEPROBE MILESTONES

History of the lonely explorers.

*Luna 1*, launched in January 1959 was the first spacecraft to leave the Earth's gravity.

In February 1966, *Luna 9* was the first craft to make a successful landing on the Moon.

*Venera 3* was the first craft to reach the surface of another planet when it crash-landed on Venus in March 1966.

*Mariner 10* was the first space probe to visit two planets (Venus and Mercury) on its mission in 1974-5.

In October 1975, *Venera 9* landed on Venus and returned the first photograph of another planet.

*Giotto*, which reached Halley's Comet in March 1986, gave us our first and only view of a cometary nucleus.

*Pioneer 10*, launched March 1972, became the first craft to leave the solar system. It continues to move away from us at 28,000 mph (45,062 km/h).

In February 2000, *NEAR (Near Earth Asteroid Rendezvous)* was the first probe to orbit and then land on an asteroid.

## 21ST CENTURY MISSIONS

- *Mars Odyssey* was launched on April 7, 2001 to make a geological survey of Mars.

- *Cassini* will reach Saturn in July 2004. It will orbit the planet and its moons for four years.

- The lander craft *Beagle 2* will arrive on Mars in December 2003, after a six-month journey on the *Mars Express* probe.

- *StarDust* will collect particles from Comet Wild-2 in early 2004, then return a capsule of material to Earth in January 2006.

- The joint Japanese and European craft *Bepi Colombo* will travel to Mercury in 2009.

- *Rosetta* will carry a lander craft to touchdown on Comet Wirtanen in 2012.

### VIEW FROM MARS

This panoramic view of the surface of Mars was composed from pictures sent back by the *Pathfinder* probe. *Pathfinder* landed on the planet on July 4, 1997.

SPACE FACTS

## KEY SPACE TELESCOPES

Space telescopes study the universe from an orbit far above the clouds and atmospheric haze that block the view of telescopes on Earth. This means that they can return the clearest possible images. Here are some notable examples:

| NAME | TYPE | IN USE | COMMENT |
|------|------|--------|---------|
| UHURU | X-ray | 1970-73 | First x-ray typ |
| IUE | Ultraviolet | 1978-96 | Long-live |
| IRAS | Infrared | 1983-83 | Surveyed 96% of sk |
| Hubble Space Telescope | Optical/UV | 1990- | Best-know |
| Rosat | UV/x-ray | 1990-99 | German and America |
| Compton Observatory | Gamma | 1991-2000 | Large |
| ISO | Infrared | 1995-98 | Europea |

## HUBBLE SPACE TELESCOPE (HST)

- The American and European telescope, the Hubble Space Telescope (HST), is an optical space telescope, which provides us with razor-sharp images of distant objects.

- The telescope is named after the American astronomer Edwin Hubble (1889-1953).

- The HST was launched on April 24, 1990 from the space shuttle *Discovery*. Its cost at launch was 2.2 billion dollars.

- It is almost the size of a bus. It measures 43.5 ft (13.2 m) by 14 ft (4. 2 m) at its widest and weighs 24,500 lb (11,110 kg ).

- The first image taken by the HST was made on May 20, 1990. It was of star cluster NGC 3532.

*Hubble is serviced from a space shuttle every two to fou years. The first servicing missio was in 1993.*

176

## DISCOVERIES

- The UHURU x-ray telescope discovered the first evidence of black holes when it recorded x-rays from the constellation Cygnus X-1.

- Ultraviolet telescopes find and watch the hottest stars – up to 50 times hotter than the Sun.

- Rosat, in space 1990-99, discovered over 1,000 very hot stars that shine briefly in ultraviolet light, as well as over 100,000 x-ray sources.

- An x-ray telescope on board *Mir* observed Supernova 1987A and found that the exploding star had created radioactive elements during the explosion.

- The Infrared Space Observatory (ISO), 1995-98, was used to observe colliding galaxies, star nurseries, and interstellar clouds.

### SPACE SNAPS

The Hubble Space Telescope provides astronomers with very clear images of the universe. This photograph of the "butterfly nebula," 2,000 light years from Earth in the constellation Monoceros, is just one example of the many beautiful color views of the cosmos that Hubble has produced.

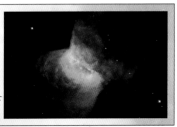

## 21ST CENTURY SPACE TELESCOPES

Space telescopes continue to be launched. Listed below are some launch dates for the current generation of space telescopes.

| NAME | LAUNCH DATE | AREA OF STUDY |
|------|-------------|---------------|
| Chandra | 1999 | High-temperature events, quasars |
| XMM Newton | 1999 | Black holes, formation of galaxies |
| HESSI | 2001 | The Sun |
| GALEX | 2001 | Galaxy evolution |
| Odin | 2001 | Molecular clouds |
| NGST | 2009 | Successor to Hubble |
| GAIA | By 2012 | Census of Milky Way stars |

# EARTH-BASED OBSERVATIONS

## OPTICAL TELESCOPES

Optical telescopes observe light from space. These are some of the most powerful optical telescopes on Earth. The first two telescopes on this list get their power by combining the light received by more than one telescope.

| NAME | LOCATION | MIRROR DIAMETER |
|---|---|---|
| Very Large Telescope (VLT) | Chile | 26.9 ft (4 x 8.2 m) |
| Large Binocular Telescope | US | 27.6 ft (2 x 8.4 m) |
| Hobby-Eberly | US | 36.1 ft (11 m) |
| Keck I | US | 32.8 ft (10 m) |
| Keck II | US | 32.8 ft (10 m) |
| Subaru | US | 27.2 ft (8.3 m) |
| Gemini North | US | 26.6 ft (8.1 m) |
| Gemini South | Chile | 26.6 ft (8.1 m) |

### SPOTS ON THE SUN

The Sun can be studied from the Earth using solar observatories. Some of these are used to record sunspots – cooler patches on the Sun's surface caused by magnetic activity beneath it.

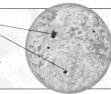

Sunspots

## RADIO TELESCOPES

Radio telescopes tune into radio waves from space. The signals they detect are turned into images by a computer. To produce a sharper image, a number of small telescopes are connected together to form an array, which can stretch over a long distance. This is a list of some of the most powerful radio telescopes in the world.

| NAME | LOCATION | SIZE |
|---|---|---|
| Arecibo | Puerto Rico | 1,000 ft (305 m) |
| Greenbank | US | 328 ft (100 m) |
| Effelsberg | Germany | 328 ft (100 m) |
| Jodrell Bank | UK | 249 ft (76 m) |
| Parkes | Australia | 210 ft (64 m) |
| Very Long Baseline Array | US | 10 dishes/4,971 miles (8,000 km) |
| Australia Telescope (array) | Australia | 8 dishes/199 miles (320 km) |
| MERLIN (array) | UK | 6 dishes/143 miles (230 km) |

## RADIO ASTRONOMY

Radio telescopes have detected some of the most energetic objects and explosive events in the universe. These include the remains of supernovas and even the radiation left over from the Big Bang.

- Radio waves with wavelengths of less than about 100 yards travel through the atmosphere to the Earth's surface. Longer radio wavelengths are reflected back into space.

- Radio astronomy began in 1932 when Karl Jansky detected radio waves coming from the Milky Way.

- The first radio waves from the Sun were picked up on British army radio sets in 1942.

- In 1949, Australian radio astronomers identified the first radio sources outside the solar system.

- Interferometry – the technique of using a number of small telescopes to act as one big one – has been used for over 50 years. This technique is able to produce much sharper results.

- Strange, radio-emitting objects were discovered in the 1950s. They were called quasistellar radio sources, or quasars.

- The first pulsar, a spinning neutron star that sends beams of radiation into space, was discovered in 1967 by Jocelyn Bell Burnell and Tony Hewish using a radio telescope.

## OPTICAL TECHNOLOGY

Professional astronomers employ the latest technology to analyze the light from space.

- Light from a star or galaxy is collected on a CCD (charge-coupled device), a stamp-sized electronic chip attached to a telescope's eyepiece end.

- A CCD can only see in black and white, so the light from an object is recorded three times, through green, blue and red filters. The three separate images are then combined to make a full-color image.

- CCDs are very sensitive. A two-minute CCD exposure shows details as faint as those in a photograph that had been exposed for an hour.

*The light-sensitive CCD chip from a large optical telescope.*

SPACE FACTS

## SPACE AND THE HUMAN BODY

- Most astronauts experience space sickness (similar to motion sickness on Earth) during their first day or two in space.

- Humidity is about 20% on board the shuttle, so humans dehydrate quickly. Astronauts drink extra water to prevent dehydration.

- Body fluids are not held down by gravity and move up to the head. In space, the face looks fatter and nasal passages become blocked.

- The spine's vertebrae float apart in the weightless conditions, making astronauts 1-2 in (2.5-5 cm) taller.

- Dust does not settle but hangs in the air. It is breathed in by astronauts, which causes them to sneeze up to 100 times a day.

- The heart doesn't need to pump as hard as it does on Earth because gravity is not pulling blood to the feet.

## SPACE TRAVELLERS

- The first living creature in space was the dog Laika. She travelled aboard *Sputnik 2* on November 3, 1957.

- Yuri Gagarin became the first human in space on April 12, 1961 when he orbited the Earth in his *Vostok 1* capsule. His trip lasted 108 minutes.

- Valentina Tereshkova, a Soviet cosmonaut, was the first woman to travel into space on June 16, 1963.

- Between 1969 and 1972, 12 astronauts traveled to the Moon in six separate missions. They spent over 300 hours on the Moon, 80 hours of which were outside their craft.

- In July 1975, Americans and Soviets linked up for the first time in space when *Apollo 18* and *Soyuz 19* docked together for two days.

- Valeri Poliakov spent 437 days, 17 hours, 58 minutes, and 16 seconds on board *Mir* in one stretch. This is the longest continuous time spent in space.

### SPACE PASSPORT

Astronauts carry a passport on space missions in case a problem forces them to land in a country that is not expecting them. This one was carried by the British astronaut Helen Sharman during her stay on *Mir*.

## LIVING IN SPACE

- Space meals are prepared from a menu of 70 foods and 20 drinks.

- A space toilet takes away waste by air suction, rather than water flush. Straps and air pressure keep the user on the seat.

- A portable vacuum cleaner is used to keep the inside of a spacecraft clean.

- To keep fit, astronauts exercise for about two hours a day, often on a treadmill.

- Astronauts sleep in tied-down sleeping bags, or bunks. Eye patches keep out the light, and special blankets suppress the noise of the equipment on board.

- Astronauts relax by listening to music, playing weightless games or taking photographs. The most popular pastime is simply looking out of the window.

## WORKING IN SPACE

- Work outside a craft is called EVA (Extra-Vehicular Activity). An astronaut is tethered to the craft, or wears an MMU (Manned Maneuvering Unit).

- The MMU, a backpack with rocket power, allows an astronaut to move freely in space, within about 328 ft (100 m) of the space craft.

- A spacesuit protects an astronaut against the temperature extremes, vacuum, and dust of space. It also provides a life-support system.

- Spacewalks can include routine tasks. The crew of *Mir* needed to clean the portholes regularly so they could see out.

- Two Soviet cosmonauts took nearly 4.5 hours to attach a new solar panel to Mir to generate extra electricity in February 1988.

# SPACE STATIONS

## SPACE STATIONS PAST AND PRESENT

Space stations orbit the Earth for several months or years, allowing astronauts to spend long periods in space. This list shows the first space stations to be launched.

| | STATION | COUNTRY | LAUNCHED | END |
|---|---|---|---|---|
| 1 | Salyut 1 | USSR | April 1971 | October 1971 |
| 2 | Salyut 2 | USSR | April 1973 | April 1973 |
| 3 | Skylab | US | May 1973 | July 1979 |
| 4 | Salyut 3 | USSR | June 1974 | August 1975 |
| 5 | Salyut 4 | USSR | December 1974 | February 1977 |
| 6 | Salyut 5 | USSR | June 1976 | August 1977 |
| 7 | Salyut 6 | USSR | September 1977 | July 1982 |
| 8 | Salyut 7 | USSR | April 1982 | February 1991 |
| 9 | Mir | USSR | February 1986 | March 2001 |
| 10 | ISS | 16 nations | November 1998 | In orbit |

## SPACE STATION MIR

- Mir was launched on February 20, 1986. Regular crew changes allowed the craft to be almost continuously occupied from March 1986 to August 1999.

- The space station orbited about 217 miles (350 km) above the Earth. It completed one orbit every 92 minutes.

- An unmanned craft called *Progress* ferried supplies such as food and water to *Mir*. It returned to Earth with waste products.

- Mir grew in size as modules were added during its lifetime. They included *Kristall*, a laboratory, and *Spektr*, an observatory.

- After 86,320 orbits, *Mir* was allowed to fall back to Earth on March 23, 2001, breaking up as it came through the atmosphere.

*The space shuttle* Atlantis *docked with Mir in June 1995.*

*This photograph shows the International Space Station in the early stages of its construction. When complete, it will cover an area the size of a football field.*

## THE INTERNATIONAL SPACE STATION (ISS)

- Construction of the ISS began on November 20, 1998 when the Russian *Zarya*, a control module, was launched on a Russian *Proton* rocket.

- The completed *International Space Station* will measure 356 ft (108.5m) wide by 290 ft (88.4 m) long by 143 ft (43.6 m) tall.

- The first crew, American astronaut Bill Shepherd and the Russians Yuri Gidzenko and Sergei Krikalev, entered the *International Space Station* on November 2, 2000.

- The ISS will be assembled from over 100 major components, including six laboratories provided by the ESA, Japan, Russia, and the United States.

- About 160 spacewalks totaling 1,920 man-hours will be made while the ISS is being assembled and maintained.

- The ISS passes over some of the Earth's most populated areas. It can observe 85% of the planet as it orbits.

## THE FUTURE OF SPACE EXPLORATION

Scientists are researching ways that space could be explored in the future. Here are some of their ideas…

- NASA and ESA (European Space Agency) scientists have developed plans to build a permanent base on the Moon.

- Vacations in space could one day be possible. Space tourists could visit a "space hotel" in the Earth's orbit or a leisure resort on the Moon.

- The ISS could be used as a "staging post" for astronauts on a mission to Mars.

- Scientists are planning to use tethers – long cables for coupling spacecraft together – as giant slingshots to accelerate craft across space.

- It is possible that future spacecraft could "sail" to the stars. Craft could be equipped with wafer-thin "sails," designed to harness pressure from the Sun's light energy. The theory is that the pressure on the sails would "push" the craft through space.

# Glossary

**ABSORPTION LINES**
Thin dark lines across a spectrum which indicate the presence of chemical elements in the light source.

**ACCRETION DISK**
A structure formed by material being drawn into a rapidly rotating black hole.

**ASTEROID**
A lump of rock orbiting the Sun. Most asteroids are found in a narrow belt situated between Mars and Jupiter.

**ASTRONAUT**
Someone who travels through space.

**ASTRONOMY**
The scientific study of objects in space.

**ATMOSPHERE**
Layer of gases surrounding a planet, moon, or star.

**AXIS (OF SPIN)**
An imaginary line through a rotating object, around which the object rotates.

**BIG BANG**
The explosion that created the universe about 15 billion years ago.

**BIG CRUNCH**
One possible future end for the universe – the Big Bang in reverse.

**BLACK HOLE**
An infinitely dense object formed initially by the collapse of a massive star. The gravity of a black hole is so strong that not even light can escape from it.

**CELESTIAL EQUATOR**
A projection of Earth's equator out into space, used as a baseline for positioning stars.

**CELESTIAL POLE**
Projection of Earth's north or south pole into space, for use as a reference point.

**CELESTIAL SPHERE**
The appearance of the stars from Earth – as though they were set into a black sphere around the planet.

**CHROMOSPHERE**
The Sun's inner atmosphere.

**CLUSTER**
A grouping of stars or galaxies held by gravity.

**COMET**
An object composed of snow and dust that orbits the Sun. If a comet approaches the Sun it forms a tail of gas and dust particles.

**CONSTELLATION**
A grouping of bright stars seen in Earth's sky. In most cases the grouping is a trick of perspective and the stars are a long way apart.

**CO-ORBITAL**
Sharing an orbital path with another object.

**CORE**
The central region of a planet, star, or galaxy.

**CORONA**
The Sun's outer atmosphere.

**CRATER**
Circular depression in the surface of a planet or a moon caused by a meteorite impact.

**CRUST**
The surface layer of a rock planet or moon.

**ECLIPSE**
The effect produced when one object in space passes in front of another and obscures it.

**ECLIPTIC**
The Sun's apparent path around the celestial sphere during a year.

**ELECTROMAGNETIC SPECTRUM**
The spectrum of radiated energy which includes: gamma rays, X-rays, ulraviolet rays, visible light, infrared radiation, microwaves, and radio and television signals.

**ESCAPE VELOCITY**
The velocity needed to overcome a planet's, or a moon's, gravity.

**FLYBY**
The path of a space probe that obtains information by flying past, or orbiting, a moon or planet.

**GALAXY**
A large grouping of stars held together by gravity. Galaxies can be spiral, elliptical (oval), or irregular in shape.

**GRAVITY**
An attractive force that is a property of mass.

**GREENHOUSE EFFECT**
Increased heating of a planetary atmosphere due to an excess of carbon dioxide.

**HELIOSPHERE**
The volume of space swept by charged particles from the Sun.

**HEMISPHERE**
One half of a sphere. The term is usually applied to regions north or south of an equator.

**LIGHT-YEAR (LY)**
The distance traveled by light in one year – used to measure distances between stars and galaxies.

**LOCAL ARM**
Name often given to the Orion arm – the spiral arm of the Milky Way galaxy in which the Sun is located.

**LOCAL GROUP**
The cluster of galaxies of which the Milky Way galaxy is a member.

**LUMINOSITY**
The amount of light energy produced by a light source.

**MAGNETIC FIELD**
The region around a magnetic source within which the magnetic force opperates.

**MAGNETOSPHERE**
The volume of space influenced by a planet's magnetic field.

**MAGNITUDE**
The brightness of a star or galaxy. Apparent magnitude is the brightness as actually seen from Earth. Absolute magnitude is the brightness if seen from a standard distance of about 32.5 light years.

**MAIN SEQUENCE**
A stage in the life cycle of stars during which they produce energy through the conversion of hydrogen to helium.

**MANTLE**
The molten middle layer of a rock planet.

**MASS**
The amount of matter in an object. The Sun's mass (1 solar mass) is used as a standard for measuring the mass of stars and galaxies.

**MATTER**
Anything that occupies space. There are three states of matter– gas, liquid, and solid.

185

**MESSIER CATALOGUE**
A list of bright clusters, galaxies, and nebulae compiled in 1781.

**METEOR**
A streak of light in the sky caused by a rock or dust particle from space burning up because of atmospheric friction.

**METEORITE**
A piece of rock or metal from space that impacts on the surface of a planet or moon.

**METEOROID**
A fragment of rock or metal in space.

**MILKY WAY**
The spiral galaxy which contains billions of stars including the Sun.

**MINOR PLANETS**
Old name for asteroids.

**MOON**
A natural satellite of a planet. Earth's moon is the Moon.

**NEBULA**
A cloud of gas and dust in space. Some nebulae glow, others are dark.

**NEUTRON STAR**
A star that has collapsed into a super-dense form of matter. Some neutron stars are seen as pulsars.

**NEW GENERAL CATALOGUE**
A list of clusters, galaxies, and nebulae first published in 1888.

**NUCLEAR FUSION**
The power source of stars. A reaction in which atoms fuse together giving off large amounts of energy.

**NUCLEUS**
The central part of an atom, comet, or galaxy.

**OBSERVATORY**
A building that contains an astronomical telescope.

**ORBIT**
The path of one object in space around another.

**ORBITAL PERIOD**
The time taken for an object to make one complete orbit.

**ORBITAL VELOCITY**
The velocity required to maintain an orbit.

**PARALLAX METHOD**
A way of calculating the distance to stars by measuring the apparent shift in their position.

**PENUMBRA**
The outer part of the shadow cast during an eclipse of the Sun. Also,

the outer and warmer part of a sunspot.

**PERIODIC COMET**
A comet that comes close to the Sun at regular intervals.

**PHOTOSPHERE**
The Sun's visible surface.

**PLANET**
A spherical object, composed of rock or liquefied gas, that orbits around a star.

**PRESSURE**
The force acting on a given area of surface.

**PROMINENCE**
A jet of gas arising from the Sun's surface.

**PROTON-PROTON CHAIN**
The main type of fusion reaction inside stars whereby hydrogen is converted into helium.

**PROTOSTAR**
A very young star that has not begun to shine.

**PULSAR**
A rapidly rotating neutron star that gives off beams of energy.

**QUASAR**
A very bright and distant object believed to be the core of a very young galaxy.

**RADAR-MAPPING**
A technique for producing relief maps from radar signals.

**RADIANT**
The point in the sky from which a meteor shower appears to come.

**RADIATION**
Forms of energy able to travel across space.

**RED GIANT**
A stage in the life cycle of many stars when they increase in size and begin the conversion of helium to carbon.

**RED SHIFT**
A shift towards the red end of the spectrum seen in light from sources that are moving away from the Earth.

**ROTATION PERIOD**
The time taken for an object to make one complete axial rotation.

**SATELLITE**
An object orbiting around a planet. There are natural satellites (moons), and artificial satellites put in orbit by human beings.

**SOLAR PANELS**
Electronic devices that produce electricity when placed in sunlight.

**SOLAR SYSTEM**
The Sun, and all the planets, moons, asteroids, and comets that orbit around it.

**SOLAR WIND**
A stream of electrically charged particles given off by the Sun.

**SPACE**
The volume between objects in the universe.

**SPECTROHELIOSCOPE**
A special telescope for studying the Sun.

**SPECTRUM**
Display of the different wavelengths or frequencies that make up radiated energy.

**STAR**
A large spinning ball of very hot gas which generates energy by nuclear fusion.

**SUNSPOTS**
Dark, irregular patches that are visible on the Sun's surface.

**SUPERCLUSTER**
A huge cluster that is itself made up of clusters of galaxies.

**SUPERNOVA**
The explosion of a large star which may briefly produce more light than an entire galaxy.

**TELESCOPE**
A device for seeing at a distance. Optical telescopes use mirrors and lenses. Radio telescopes use metal dishes to "see" radio signals. Other telescopes are sensitive to other forms of energy.

**UMBRA**
The inner part of the shadow cast during a solar or lunar eclipse. Also, the inner and cooler part of a sunspot.

**UNIVERSE**
Everything that exists.

**VACUUM**
Space empty of matter.

**WAVELENGTH**
A characteristic feature of radiant energy.

**WEIGHTLESSNESS**
Condition of apparent zero gravity experienced by space travelers.

**WHITE DWARF**
The collapsed core of a Sun-sized star.

**ZODIAC**
The 12 constellations through which the Sun appears to travel during one year.

# Index

# Acknowledgements

**Dorling Kindersley would like to thank:**
Caroline Potts for sympathetic photo-librarianship, Robert Graham , Ray Rogers and Connie Mersel for cheerful assistance, Hilary Bird for the index, and Dr. David W. Hughes of Sheffield University for his much appreciated professional advice.

**Illustrations by:**
Rick Blakely, Luciano Corbella, Richard Draper, Mike Grey, Jeremy Gower, John Hutchinson, Andrew Macdonald, J. Marffy, Daniel J. Pyne, Pete Serjeant, Guy Smith, Taurus Graphics, Raymond Turvey, François Vincent, Richard Ward, Brian Watson,  John Woodcock

**Picture credits:**  t = top b = bottom c = centre l = left r = right
Anglo Australian Telescope Board/D.Malin 35tr, 40/41, Rob Beighton 81cl, The Bodleian Library, University of Oxford 140bl, ESO/Meylan 124tr, 128b, 135tl, 137t, Mary Evans Picture Library 140cl, 141tr, 141crb, 141br, 142tl; FLPA 44tr, Genesis Space Photo Library 8/9, 125t, Harvard University Archives 144t, Image Select/Ann Ronan 142b,143t, JPL courtesy of NOAO 110tl, Lund Observatory 23tl, Mansell Collection

141rct, 142tc, NASA/JPL 11tr, 14bl, 18tl, 19tr, 22tr, 25tr, 26/27, 28tr, 30tr, 52tr, 58/59, 64tr, 66bl, 68/69, 70tr, 71tl, 74tr, 75tr, 77tl, 78tl, 79tl, 82tl, 83tl, 86tr, 87tr, 88cl, 90tr, 91tr, 94tr, 95tr, 96cl, 98tr, 99bl, 102tr, 103tr, 104cl, 106tr, 116/117, 119tr, 119cr, 124b, 125c, 125b, 128tr, 130tr, 131cl, 132tr, 134tr, 136tr, 136br, 137cr, 137bl, 138/139, 142clb, 145cb, 146/147, 147cl, 148cr, Novosti 149tl, Science Photo Library/ Alex Bariel 120tr, Dr Jeremy Burgess 140tl, ESA 111br, Fred Espenak 43t, François Gohier 122tr, Max Planck Institut fur Radioastronomy 122bl, 144b, David Mclean 112tr, NASA 114tr, NOAO 16/17, 119c, Pekka Parviaimen 45tl, Roger Ressmeyer, Starlight 42tr, Royal Observatory Edinburgh/Anglo-Australian Telescope Board 20tr, 24bl, 48tr, 108/109; Royal Greenwich Observatory 123cl, John Sanford 46tr, 113br, Dr. Seth Shostak 123tl, Starland Picture Library/ESO 33tl, UPI/Bettman 144cr.

Every effort has been made to trace the copyright holders and we apologise in advance for any unintentional omissions. We would be pleased to insert the appropriate acknowledgment in any subsequent edition of this publication.